DATE DUE

NOV 08 1996		
FE 24 '97		
MAY 16 1997		
OCT 28 1998		
JAN 28 1999		
JA 27 '00		
GAYLORD		PRINTED IN U.S.A.

CULTURES OF THE WORLD

ARGENTINA

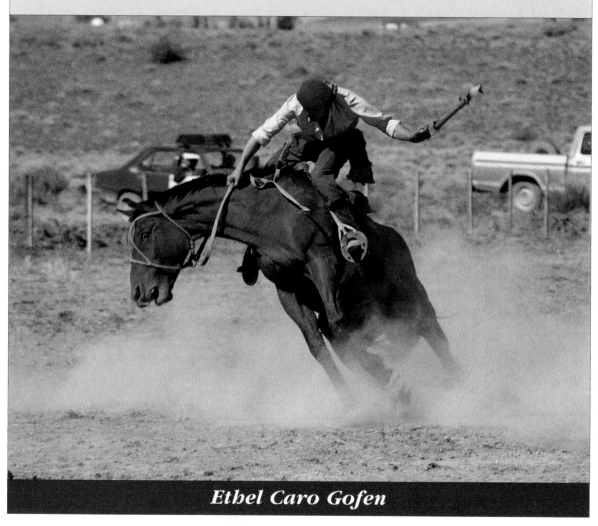

Ethel Caro Gofen

MARSHALL CAVENDISH
New York • London • Sydney

Reference edition published 1992 by
Marshall Cavendish Corporation
2415 Jerusalem Avenue
North Bellmore
New York 11710

Editorial Director	Shirley Hew
Managing Editor	Shova Loh
Editors	Roseline Lum
	Siow Peng Han
	Leonard Lau
	MaryLee Knowlton
Picture Editor	Jane Duff
Production	Edmund Lam
Design	Tuck Loong
	Lee Woon Hong
	Dani Phoa
	Ong Su Ping
	Katherine Tan
Illustrator	Thomas Koh

Printed in Singapore

Library of Congress Cataloging-in-Publication Data:
Gofen, Ethel, 1937–
    Argentina / Ethel Gofen.
      p. cm.—(Cultures Of The World)
    Includes bibliographical references.
    Summary: Profiles the history, geography,
      government, and people of Argentina, and
      highlights the country's main cultural and
      social traditions.
    ISBN 1 85435 524 4
    1. Argentina. [1. Argentina.] I. Title. II. Series.
F2808.2.G64 1991
982—dc20   90-23159
                       CIP

INTRODUCTION

The Argentina of the romantic imagination is a land of spectacular scenery, colorful cowboys called gauchos, dramatic tango dancers, polo players, and soccer champions. The real Argentina has all these plus a sophisticated culture centered in Buenos Aires and a stormy history dominated by charismatic, often controversial, leaders.

The name Argentina means "silver," and this fertile country has long fostered explorers' dreams of unlimited wealth. Political strife and the harsh economic realities of the past 50 years have deferred those dreams. What lingers is the exceptional beauty of the country, the pride of its highly educated citizens, and their enduring wish to attain for their country its destined greatness in world culture and affairs.

This book, part of the series *Cultures of the World,* will provide insights into the extreme diversity of Argentina's people and their lifestyles.

CONTENTS

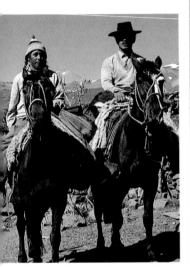

Argentina is blessed with a beautiful countryside, friendly people and a colorful culture.

CONTENTS

Argentina: Land of heroes and legends from an exciting and glorious past.

5

GEOGRAPHY

WHETHER YOU DREAM OF mountain peaks, sandy beaches, or fertile plains, the vast South American country of Argentina has them all. Its terrain stretches from the subtropical north to sub-Antarctic regions of the south.

One major reason its climate and geography are so dramatically diverse is that the country is so long—about 2,300 miles. Since it lies in the Southern Hemisphere, the climate in general is hottest in the north, nearer the Equator, and coldest in the south.

Argentina is the eighth largest country in the world. In South America, only Brazil is larger in area and population. The land mass of Argentina covers almost 1.1 million square miles, measuring 868 miles across at its broadest point.

Argentina's neighbors are Bolivia and Paraguay to the north, Brazil and Uruguay to the east, and Chile to the south and west. The Atlantic Ocean on the east and south and the snow-capped Andes Mountains on the west form long stretches of natural borders.

As a country with long stretches of mountains and seashore, Argentina boasts of some famous extremes of elevation. The Salinas Grandes, or Great Salt Mines, is the lowest place on the South American continent—131 feet below sea level. Near the Chilean border the summit of Mt. Aconcagua, an extinct volcano, is the highest spot in the Western Hemisphere (22,831 feet).

Opposite: **The Perito Moreno Glacier in Patagonia. Glaciers are actually very large blocks of ice.**

Below: **The desert of northwest Argentina. The country has one of the most diverse climatic variations in the world.**

NORTHERN ARGENTINA

The northern part of Argentina is heavily forested, low, wet and hot. Early settlers called one area of the north the Gran Chaco, or hunting ground, to distinguish it from the pampas, a vast cattle grazing region further south.

Few people live in the forests of the Chaco. This region is rich in forest products, but its fertility is limited in some parts by swamps and in other spots by periodic dry spells. Winters in the Chaco are dry, while summers are very humid, with temperatures rising as high as 120°. Yearly rainfall ranges from 60 inches in the northeast to 20 inches in the west.

Another part of the north is called Mesopotamia, which includes the province of Entre Ríos. Both names mean "between rivers." These lowlands lie between the Paraná and Uruguay rivers. Rolling grassy plains, rivers and swamps are their chief features. The climate is warm and wet all year round. Ranchers raise cattle, horses and sheep here. Farmers grow flax, wheat and fruit.

The Misiones province in north-eastern Mesopotamia has heavy rains, thick forests and many waterfalls. The most spectacular is the dramatic Iguazú Falls on the Brazilian border. The region's most famous crop is the holly plant, used for *yerba maté*. This brewed herbal tea, the gaucho's favorite drink, is now served all over Argentina.

Palm savannahs on the wet and swampy lowlands of Entre Ríos.

IGUAZU FALLS: WORLD-CLASS TOURIST DESTINATION

Misiones, in northeastern Mesopotamia, is covered by lush tropical rainforests and colorful wildlife. But the most spectacular scenery is the dramatic Iguazú Falls on the Brazilian border. Imagine the thrill of being the first Spanish explorer to discover this gorgeous cascade in 1541.

Iguazú is a Guaraní Indian word meaning Great Water. More than 275 waterfalls stretch around an 8,100-foot-wide arc of the Río Iguazú. They fall roughly 270 feet and splash over a series of islands, creating spectacular sprays and rainbows. The largest waterfall, called the Devil's Throat, is more than 350 feet high.

The falls are set in a national park with 132,500 acres of tropical jungle. A wildlife reserve shelters hundreds of species of birds, reptiles, fish, 25 species of butterflies, orchids, monkeys, parrots and pumas. Nature lovers also appreciate the hundreds of different species of trees and tropical plants.

A Hollywood film, *The Mission*, set at Iguazú Falls, showed vivid scenes of the life of native Indians, Jesuit priests and Spanish colonials 200 years ago. It won the 1986 Cannes Film Festival Best Picture award and an Oscar for Best Cinematography.

The early history of the Argentinean pampas was much like the Wild West in North America. The gauchos, Argentina's cowboys, rode horseback and herded cattle in the pampas.

THE PAMPAS

More than two-thirds of Argentina's people live in the pampas. Most cities, industries and important transportation facilities are also in this part of the country. The capital, Buenos Aires, and several other large cities are located here. Argentina's wealth comes mainly from this region.

The pampas are flat, fertile, and temperate plains in the central part of the country. They stretch from the Atlantic Ocean to the Andes, covering one-fifth of Argentina.

The word "pampas" comes from a Guaraní Indian word meaning Level Land. Visitors are astounded when they see these plains stretching endlessly to the horizon in all directions, with barely a tree or stone to catch the eye, and as flat as the sea. While there is plenty of rain in the eastern part, about 40 inches per year, the climate becomes drier to the west. Much of the country's chief crops—wheat, corn, and alfalfa—are raised in its rich soil. Vast herds of cattle graze on the drier western plains. Farmers also raise flax and hogs here.

THE ANDES

The western part of Argentina, bordering on Chile, is marked by the huge mountain range of the Andes. Not many people live in this rugged area. A small group of Indians raise sheep in the northern part of the Argentinean Andes. Miners dig for iron ore, uranium, and other metals. Although the earliest Spanish settlements were in the Andes, today only about 15% of the people live here.

Just east of the Andes is a region called the Piedmont. In these low mountains and desert valleys, farmers grow important crops, especially sugarcane, corn, cotton and fruit for export.

Most Argentinean wines come from the vineyards near Mendoza and the grapes of San Juan in the Piedmont. The dry climate, sandy soil, and year-round sunshine are ideal for the wine industry.

West of Mendoza lies Mt. Aconcagua, meaning Stone Guard in an Indian dialect.

Just south of this highest peak of the Western Hemisphere is the Uspallata Pass, the Camino de los Andes. This pass leads into Chile at a height of 12,600 feet.

Mt. Aconcagua is the highest mountain in South America.

THE SOUTHERNMOST TOWN IN THE WORLD

The southernmost town in the world, Ushuaia (an Indian word pronounced "oos-why'-uh"), is situated in Argentina. Its weather is almost always chilly, and the nearby mountains are usually snow-capped. The 20,000 people of Ushuaia can look south across the waters of the Beagle Channel

toward the South Pole, some 650 miles away. Like people who live in other parts of southern Patagonia and the Tierra del Fuego, folks in Ushuaia have only about seven hours of daylight in the winter. In the summer, they enjoy daylight for about 17 hours each day.

PATAGONIA

Patagonia covers more than a fourth of Argentina, and includes windswept dry plateaus crossed by many deep canyons. It lies in the rain shadow of the Andes, resulting in stretches of cool desert.

Beautiful resort areas of lakes and mountains are in the west, while it is always cool and often foggy, with many storms, in the far south. Although there is no real summer, ocean currents keep winter

Except where the government has built irrigation canals, most of Patagonia has such poor soil and little rainfall that crops cannot grow there.

temperatures moderate. At the southern tip of South America is the island of Tierra del Fuego, or Land of Fire. It was named for the Ona and Yagane Indian campfires seen by early European sailors. Soon European settlers and Chileans arrived to raise sheep on large ranches and grow vegetables and fruit on irrigated farms. Only about 1–3% of Argentina's population live in Patagonia. It made a perfect hideout for the legendary bank robbers from North America— Butch Cassidy and the Sundance Kid, and Etta.

"The Argentine lake region ... is cold, the vegetation ancient; silent and solitary forests end at silent lakes that mirror snowy hills resplendent in the sun."

—*Argentinean writer Jorge Luis Borges.*

ARGENTINA'S WATERS

More than 1,600 miles of the length of Argentina are bounded by the Atlantic Ocean. Several large bays dot the seacoast. The most important is formed by the Río de la Plata, the longest river in Argentina, which flows between Argentina and Uruguay.

The Paraná River system drains northern and much of central Argentina. The giant rivers in Argentina serve as boundaries and as important transportation arteries.

The drainage patterns of Argentina's rivers and lakes are greatly affected by the height of the Andean mountains. In the south, a series of Argentinean lakes empty into the Pacific Ocean through Chile. But after heavy rains, they send their extra water into the Atlantic Ocean. This happens because the lakes sit almost directly on top of the continental divide, a line that separates waters flowing east from those flowing west.

A lake noted for its special beauty is Nahuel Huapí. It extends for 200 square miles at 2,500 feet above sea level at the heart of a nature reserve and resort area in the southern Andes. A natural feature of great interest to visitors is the Perito Moreno Glacier in Patagonia. The glacier moves five yards a day, noisily shattering icebergs in its path and raising a dramatic explosion of spray.

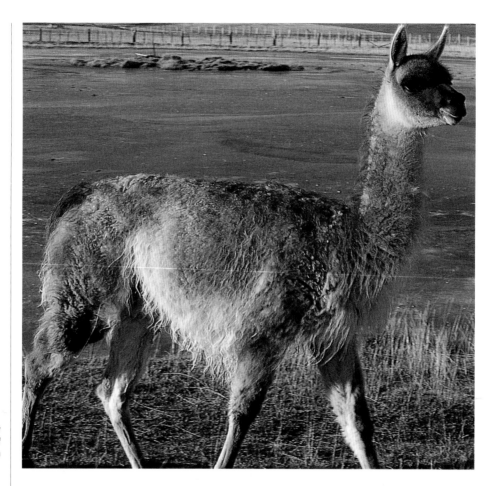

The llama is commonly found in the highlands of the northern Andean plateau.

COLORFUL WILDLIFE

Unusual animals that live in Argentina include the armadillo, opossum, coatimundi, tapir, jaguar, howler monkey, giant anteater and puma.

The guanaco is a small relation to the camel that, unlike its larger cousin, has no hump. It is the common ancestor of the llama, alpaca and vicuña. These animals roam the northern Andean plateau. The alpaca and vicuña contribute hides and wool to the economy.

The Patagonian cavy is related to the guinea pig. The vizcacha, a burrowing animal of the pampas, digs far-ranging underground tunnels that trip the horses and cattle. And the capybara is the world's largest rodent, sometimes weighing more than 110 pounds.

Visitors to Patagonia are impressed by the picturesque wildlife of the coasts: dolphins, penguins and sealions. The Valdés Peninsula, a large nature reserve on the Atlantic coast, has herds of huge elephant seals, rheas (large ostrich-like birds), guanacos and many other interesting birds and animals.

Argentinean birds include flamingos, herons, parrots, the black-necked swans, and the crested screamers. There are also the tinamou, a relative of the ostrich; the albatross (a large, web-footed seabird) and the cóndor, a huge vulture in danger of extinction.

THE WORLD'S OLDEST DINOSAUR

In November 1989, a scientist from the University of Chicago revealed an amazing discovery. In 1988, in northwestern Argentina, his team had spotted a full skeleton of the most ancient dinosaur yet found. They named it *Herrerasaurus* to honor Victorino Herrera, the goat farmer who led scientists to the bones.

This dinosaur lived 230 million years ago. At that time, scientists believe, most of the earth's land was part of a single supercontinent called Pangea. This meat-eating dinosaur was about six feet long and weighed 300 pounds. It had sharp teeth like a shark's, talons like an eagle's, and back legs like those of an ostrich.

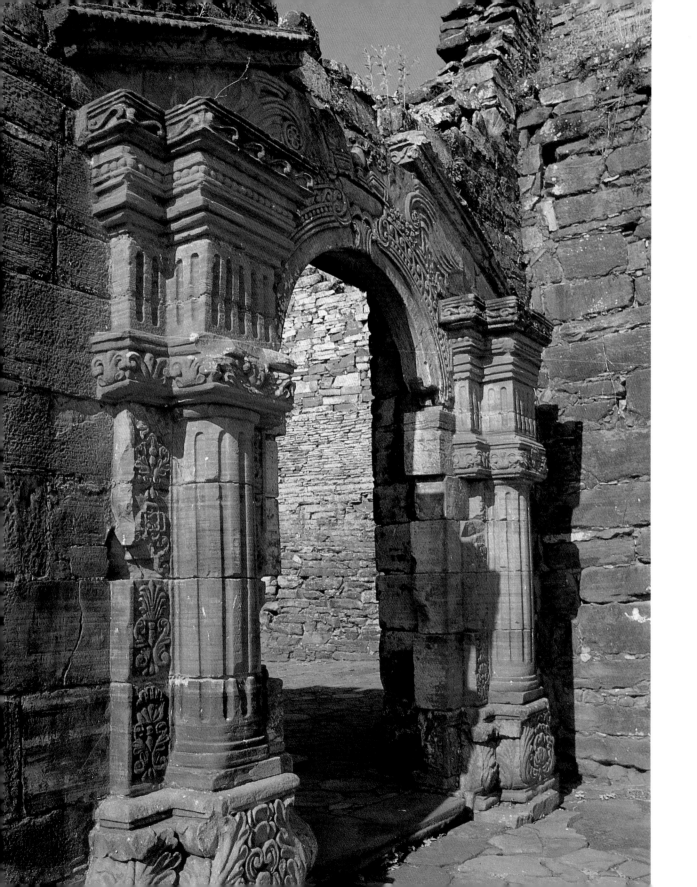

HISTORY

THE INDIAN EMPIRES The first people in Argentina were the Indians of the Americas. They were hunters and food gatherers. Like the Indians of North America, they may have descended from Asia, crossing the Bering Strait from Siberia in prehistoric times.

When the first Europeans arrived, some 300,000 Indians were occupying the land that eventually became Argentina. A combination of war, diseases such as smallpox and measles, interbreeding, and destruction by the colonists greatly reduced the Indian population. Today only about 50,000 full-blooded Indians remain.

EXPLORERS FROM EUROPE The first European to land in Argentina was reportedly the Portuguese explorer Juan Díaz de Solís, in 1516. He sailed into the Río de la Plata estuary and claimed the land for Spain. (Solís was killed and eaten by Indians on another landing venture in South America.) Four years later, Portuguese explorer Ferdinand Magellan stopped at the same river on his historic voyage around the world.

In 1526, Sebastian Cabot, an Italian serving Spain, founded the first European settlement, later abandoned, near the present city of Rosario. Cabot named the Río de la Plata, or River of Silver, for the silver jewelry the Indians were wearing.

Opposite: **The San Ignacio ruins in Misiones where Jesuits worked to convert the Indians to Christianity.**

Below: **The Indians were the original settlers of the land. The desire of new immigrants to cultivate the land wiped out most of the Indian settlements.**

The Cabildo in Buenos Aires. This used to be the council building for the colonial government.

THE COLONIAL PERIOD The history of Argentina is part of the larger story of conquest and subsequent settling of South America by Spanish and Portuguese colonists. The conquest of the Inca Empire of Peru in 1532 by Francisco Pizarro opened the way for these colonists.

Most of the Spaniards who arrived by sea were eventually driven away by Indians and by the threat of starvation. The Spanish colonists who finally settled in Argentina came mainly over the mountains from Peru and Chile. That is how Argentina's oldest cities such as Jujuy, Salta, Tucumán, Mendoza and Córdoba were founded in the latter half of the 16th century. Buenos Aires was permanently established in 1580.

Horses, sheep and cattle brought from Spain thrived and multiplied in the new land. During the 17th century, the Spanish government needed money and began to sell large plots of land to private owners. This led to the establishment of huge estates owned by rich Europeans and *criollos*, or people of European descent born in Latin America. To herd their semi-wild cattle, the owners hired gauchos, or cowboys, who were usually *mestizos,* people of mixed Indian and Spanish blood.

José de San Martín is also known as El Libertador (the liberator) for his leadership in the fight for independence from Spain. His statues dominate the main squares of cities, towns, and villages throughout Argentina. His portrait hangs in every state school and decorates the postage stamps.

INDEPENDENCE In time, the rich landowners began to resent the Spanish government's interference in their business affairs. The landowners grew more powerful. They wanted to control trade and keep more of the wealth they produced at home rather than send it back to Spain. They yearned for independence.

When France attacked Spain in Europe (1807–08), Buenos Aires seized on that opportunity to fight for its independence. On May 25, 1810, Argentina broke away from its motherland, but King Ferdinand of Spain did not recognize the independence of the new colony.

The Argentinean national hero, General José de San Martín, urged Argentinean leaders to formally declare independence from Spain. This occurred in Tucumán on July 9, 1816, and the new country was called the United Provinces of the River Plate.

San Martín then led a famous expedition across the Andes into Chile and helped drive out the Spanish troops there and in Peru. Spain's domination of the South American continent finally ended.

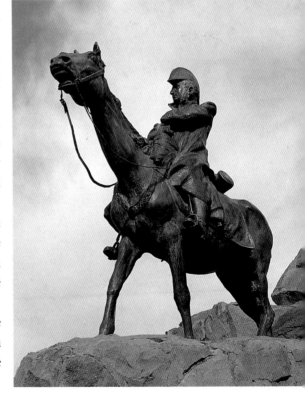

FORGING A NATION

The next 50 years were marked by two major forces: (1) the struggle between Buenos Aires and the provinces, and (2) political turmoil under different kinds of government. The *porteños,* or residents of the port city of Buenos Aires, quarreled with ranchers in the provinces over control of the country's rural areas. These conflicts almost destroyed trade and the entire economy.

The tyrant, Juan Manuel de Rosas—president from 1829 to 1852.

A constitution drawn in 1826 gave Buenos Aires control over the interior. The first president of Argentina, Bernardino Rivadavia, was a *porteño.* He was soon overthrown by the rival political party of the rural ranchers. Their leader was in turn assassinated by members of Rivadavia's party.

The next ruler was a type that would appear frequently in Argentinean history—the strongman, or *caudillo.* Juan Manuel de Rosas, a landowner from the pampas, ruled Argentina as a dictator from 1829 to 1852. He persecuted and murdered many of his political enemies and wiped out a great number of Indians. Rosas was finally overthrown by General Justo José de Urquiza and escaped to England, where he spent the rest of his life in comfortable exile.

FROM 1853 TO 1880

The constitution proclaimed in 1853 was patterned after that of the United States. Urquiza became president of a new confederation of the provinces.

In 1860, Argentina officially adopted its present name, from *argentum,* the Latin word for "silver." The province of Buenos Aires alone refused to join the confederation until 1862, after several battles. Buenos Aires became the nation's capital, and General Bartolomé Mitre took over as president of the 14 united provinces of the Argentine Republic.

In this period of rapid changes, another president, Domingo Faustino Sarmiento (1868–74), vigorously promoted public education in Argentina. The country to this day has one of the highest literacy rates in the world.

The war between the settlers and the Indians in Tierra del Fuego during the 1880s.

In 1880, Buenos Aires became a federal district, something like the District of Columbia in the United States.

The pressure for more grazing land resulted in the Indian Wars of the late 1870s and early 1880s. During these battles, the Indian tribes in the pampas and Patagonia were virtually exterminated. Their lands were taken over by the officers who led the campaign against them.

THE GOLDEN AGE

Some historians call the years from 1880 until the outbreak of the First World War in 1914 "The Golden Age" of Argentina. Huge numbers of immigrants and amounts of foreign investment arrived from Europe. Argentina seemed a land of natural resources and frontier wilderness during the early 20th century, destined to become one of the world's richest and greatest nations. The railroad system expanded rapidly. Refrigerated ships began to carry beef and hides to Europe in 1877, and exports of farm products grew rapidly. Sheep farming became more important. By the 1880s, wool constituted half the value of Argentina's exports.

During this period, streets were paved, broad avenues and parks were built, and majestic public buildings and private homes sprang up. Argentina became the most urbanized country in Latin America.

In 1929, the Great Depression triggered by the United States stock market crash affected Argentina along with many other countries of the world. As the Argentinean economy declined sharply, army leaders threw the president out of office in 1930 and began a series of military dictatorships. Argentina remained neutral throughout most of the Second World War (1939–45). War was finally declared on Germany and Japan in March 1945.

Argentina attracted many immigrants, such as the owner of this pharmacy, in the early 20th century.

THE PERON ERA

The most famous strongman leader in Argentina's history, Colonel Juan Domingo Perón, rose to power while generals ran the government in the 1940s. He served as a minister of labor in a *junta* (group of military leaders) government, then became president in 1946. He appealed to the workers by giving them higher wages, pensions and other benefits, and by strengthening their unions. His supporters formed the Peronist party, which remains influential to this day.

Before Perón, foreign countries had tremendous power over Argentina's economy. The British controlled most of the railroads. The United States controlled the auto business. Even the meat-packing industry was dominated by foreigners. Perón increased government spending, took control of many of the country's industries, and built up manufacturing at the expense of farm production, which he taxed heavily. The resulting drop in farm production caused the national income to fall.

Civil liberties eroded under Perón. He suspended freedom of the press and of speech, altered the constitution to increase his powers, and permitted a second term of office for himself. He remained popular with some Argentineans because of his charm and appeal to their national pride. But during his second term, his power and popularity declined. He lost the support of the Catholic Church and even alienated the army and navy. Perón fled in 1955 and eventually settled in Spain, leaving Argentina nearly bankrupt. His legacy of large debts and huge inflation stayed, yet his ideas continue to appeal to many.

"For people like me, Perón was and still is a prophet, a visionary, a father-figure."
—*Luis Manzano*

Juan Domingo Perón

23

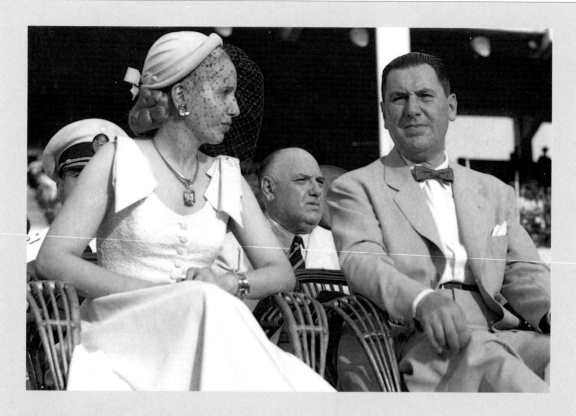

EVITA PERON

Perón's beautiful second wife, Eva Duarte de Perón (Evita), a former actress, was a powerful leader in her own right until her early death at 33 from cancer. She was idolized by the urban working class. She gained the right to vote for women in 1947 and founded women's political and social-service organizations. Her work brought health and welfare benefits to the poor. The masses expressed their affection for Evita in huge demonstrations. For many, her magnificent jewels and gowns and her rags-to-riches story symbolized a proud and wealthy Argentina.

Evita was born in the poor village of Los Toldos in 1919. She went to Buenos Aires in her teens and became a popular radio actress. Perón, a widower, was 48 and she was 24 when they met. She greatly assisted his rise to power, and his popularity dropped after her death. Many Argentineans viewed Evita as a near-saint, but the Catholic Church in Rome resisted all pressure to canonize her. Her epitaph reads, "Don't cry for me, Argentina, I remain quite near to you."

DISRUPTION

Military dictators and civilian presidents alternated during the years of Perón's exile. In 1956, Perón's constitution of 1949 was replaced with the original constitution of 1853. Peronists were banned from political activity. The most noted president of this period was Arturo Frondizi (1958–62), who helped industrialize Argentina. He tried unsuccessfully to lower the debt and reduce inflation.

After a period of strikes and political unrest, the military allowed a Peronist named Héctor José Cámpora to become president in 1973. Later that year, Perón returned from his Spanish exile. Cámpora resigned, enabling Perón to be elected president once more in October 1973. He governed briefly until his death the following year at the age of 79.

After Perón's death, Isabel, his third wife, became the first woman president in the Western Hemisphere. Incredible inflation—over 400%—and terrorist violence plagued the country. Kidnapings, bombings, and executions of military officers, businessmen, and newspaper publishers were the work of the guerrilla group, the left-wing Montoneross.

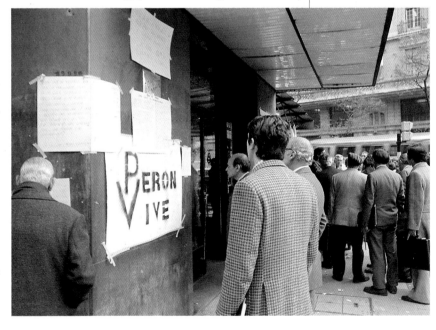

After being suppressed by the military dictatorship for many years, the Peronist party returned to power with the support and vote of the people.

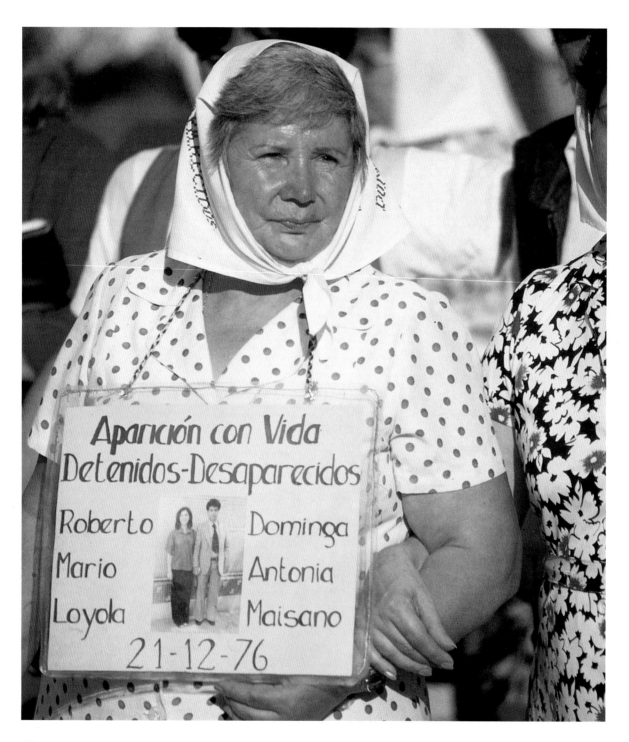

THE "DIRTY WAR"

In 1976, military leaders arrested Isabel Perón. They seized the government, dissolved the Congress, outlawed all political parties, censored the press, and banned all strikes. These leaders began a *guerra sucia,* or "dirty war," against the terrorists.

They did succeed in destroying the power of the guerrilla groups, but in their campaign they condoned violence against thousands. The government often made its enemies disappear by kidnaping and killing them and never revealing what happened to them afterward.

Mothers and grandmothers of the "disappeared" began to demonstrate in the Plaza de Mayo, outside the government headquarters every Thursday afternoon. Later investigations revealed that most of the "disap-

Opposite and below: **The Mothers of the Plaza de Mayo. A report published in 1986 lists almost 9,000 cases of people who disappeared during the "dirty war." The real numbers, however, will never be known.**

peared" had been murdered. Hundreds of detention centers had been used to imprison, torture, and kill people. Mass graves were discovered. A government commission later called the military campaign against terrorists and dissidents the "greatest tragedy of our history, and the most savage."

The Falkland Islands are remote and desolate, inhabited by about 2,000 people in 1984. The islands' economy relies solely on sheep farming.

THE FALKLANDS WAR AND DEMOCRACY

Argentina's economy continued to decline, especially during the period of the Falklands War in 1982. Both Britain and Argentina claimed ownership of these islands, which Argentina calls the Islas Malvinas. They lie about 300 miles off the coast of Argentina and are occupied by British citizens.

President Leopoldo Galtieri, an army general, had hoped to unite the people behind his military government by occupying these islands. Argentinean troops fought in the air, at sea, and on the islands but failed to oust the British. The Argentinean army never expected such a strong retaliation from Great Britain when they occupied the islands. The war lasted 72 tragic days and cost 2,000 Argentinean and British lives.

When Argentina surrendered, it did not give up its claim to the islands. Britain keeps a 2,500-man garrison in the Falklands. It took seven years after the war for Argentina and Great Britain to resume consular ties, air and sea links, and unrestricted trade.

This military defeat led to the call for free elections in October 1983. Raúl Alfonsín became president in December of that year and Argentina fully restored its constitution of 1853.

Alfonsín tried to bring to justice some of the military commanders who had violated human rights during the "dirty war." Nine commanders were tried, and five received prison sentences. The military was able to prevent the prosecution of lower-ranking officers who, they said, were only following orders.

The short Falklands War further crippled Argentina's weak economy and cost the lives of many British and Argentinean soldiers.

Eventually, economic woes—inflation, unemployment, and falling wages—damaged Alfonsín's popularity. On May 14, 1989, Carlos Saúl Menem of the union-backed Peronist party was elected president. Riots over high food prices led Alfonsín to resign on June 30, allowing Menem to take office five months early.

Menem campaigned as a candidate of a party that traditionally stood for big government, big benefits and big deficits. Once in office, he surprised his constituents by pushing for freer markets and a reduced role for government. His biggest challenge remains Argentina's inflation.

GOVERNMENT

ARGENTINA'S OFFICIAL NAME is República Argentina (Argentine Republic). It was established as a republic on May 1, 1853, when the constitution was adopted. Parts of the Argentinean constitution were modeled after that of the United States. It calls for an elected president and congress. The president and vice president must be born in Argentina and must be Catholics. They serve a six-year term and cannot be immediately re-elected.

Power is divided among the executive, legislative and judicial branches of the government. This creates a system of checks and balances that is supposed to prevent one person or branch from gaining complete control of the nation.

The president appoints a cabinet of ministers to head the executive departments of the government. The vice president leads the Senate and becomes president if the president can no longer serve.

The Congress is made up of two houses, the Chamber of Deputies and the Senate. The larger Chamber of Deputies has 254 members elected directly by the people. Deputies serve for four years. The Senate comprises 46 members chosen by the local legislatures. Two senators come as representatives of each of the 22 provinces, and two from the Federal District of Buenos Aires. Senators serve for nine years.

In addition to its 22 provinces and one federal district, Argentina includes the island territory of Tierra del Fuego. The people in each province can elect a governor, but the president appoints the governor of Tierra del Fuego. The Federal District is run by a mayor appointed by the president. Everyone aged 18 and above can vote in the elections.

Opposite: **A Presidential Guard outside the Casa Rosada.**

Above: **Argentina has two main political parties: the Radical Civic Union or the Radical Party, which attracts many middle-class voters, and the Justicialist Liberation Front, also called the Peronist Party.**

THE JUDICIARY

The Argentinean system of courts and judges—the judiciary—has been influenced by the systems used in the United States and Western Europe. The president appoints the members of the Supreme Court and also the judges of the Federal Courts of Appeals. All Supreme Court and federal judges are appointed for life.

To ensure that justice and the law are impartially applied to all, judges in Argentina are appointed for life.

Each province has its own system of lower and higher courts. Judges in the provinces are appointed by the local governors. Local governments have limited powers, however, due to the fact that the president of Argentina can remove the governor of a province and call for new elections to fill that seat.

The constitution establishes trial by jury for criminal cases, but it is rarely practiced. The death penalty was re-introduced in 1976 more as a deterrent than as punishment for the killing of government, military police and judicial officials, and for terrorist activities. By 1990, it was no longer being used.

THE ARMED FORCES WIELD GREAT POWER

The president is commander-in-chief of the armed forces. Men from the ages of 18 to 45 must spend 12 months or more in the army or the air force, or a minimum of 14 months in the navy. Women may hold non-fighting jobs in the armed forces.

At times, the armed forces have been Argentina's strongest political force. Military leaders have made and overthrown governments many times during this century. Some military coups have been bloody, while others were less violent.

No Argentinean president in the 20th century could achieve goals or even remain long in office without the support of the military. Military takeovers often affected constitutional governments in Argentina, but only once was the constitution actually set aside.

The constitution of 1853 guaranteed the people freedom of speech and religion and gave them the right of public assembly and private property. These and other civil liberties guaranteed by the constitution often suffered under military regimes.

The great task in governing Argentina has been to develop a stable government that will not be overthrown whenever it displeases some powerful group in the country.

The House of Congress. In a democratic and civilian government, the country's armed forces has reverted to its role of defending the country, not ruling it.

CARLOS SAUL MENEM

The current president of Argentina, Carlos Saúl Menem, was born in Argentina. He is a Catholic, as required by law, but he comes from a Syrian-Arab Moslem family.

President Carlos Saúl Menem set out to tackle Argentina's serious economic problems after his 1989 election.

Menem was elected president on May 14, 1989. He belongs to the Justicialist Liberation Front Party. He had been a popular governor of the economically-depressed province of La Rioja in the northwest. As a representative of the Peronist movement, Menem's campaign appealed to the workers and the poor.

Menem often makes headlines because of his flamboyant personality. He has toured Argentina in a luxury bus and been featured in magazines wearing bathing suits. He likes to fly planes and play soccer with the country's leading athletes.

Like the most famous wife of a president in Argentinean history, Evita Perón, Mrs. Menem is a striking blonde. But unlike Evita, Zulema Yoma de Menem is no help to her husband in politics. President Menem and his wife have battled openly. Newspapers headlined the time when he had her locked out of the official residence. She has publicly voiced her support for Menem's political opponents. Unlike her husband, a Catholic convert, Mrs. Menem retains her Moslem religion.

THE STATE FLAG AND
THE COAT OF ARMS

The sun with a human face, called the "Sun of May," appears on the state flag (adopted 1818) and on the coat of arms. It stands for Argentina's freedom from Spain. The colors, light blue and white, were worn by Argentineans who fought off British invaders in 1806 and 1807.

The coat of arms shows two hands clasped and surrounded by a laurel wreath. In the back is a red "liberty cap" on a pole. On top of the wreath is the rising sun. The light blue and white colors match those of the flag.

ECONOMY

THE SPANISH EXPLORERS named Argentina for the precious silver they were seeking in the new land. But they didn't find much of it. Instead, they brought cattle from Europe and later sheep, and they cultivated wheat. These were the bases for Argentina's economic growth.

Argentina is potentially one of the most prosperous countries in Latin America. Food is plentiful and cheap. The poverty, starvation, and malnutrition that plague many other countries on the continent are almost unknown in Argentina.

Half of Argentina's total land area is used for pasture. In the roughly 12% of the land that is cultivated for crops, the soil is richly productive. The main farm crops include corn, wheat, soybeans and sorghum. Grapes, apples, citrus fruits, sugarcane, *yerba maté*, tobacco, cotton, and tea are also grown. From the grapes come a variety of wines.

Argentina is famous for its beef production. The British cattle breeds of Aberdeen Angus, Hereford and Shorthorn, and the French Charolais are particularly popular. Patagonia and other dry areas are key regions of sheep-breeding, with sheep's wool being another major export item. Argentinean farmers raise large numbers of hogs and poultry. The dairy industry is also extensive.

About 15% of the work force is employed in agriculture, which accounts for 9% of Argentina's gross national product, or GNP. The GNP measures the total amount of goods and services produced by a country.

Opposite and below: **Early explorers expected to find huge silver deposits in Argentina. The wealth they did find consisted of rich soil and vast stretches of grazing land for cattle.**

Argentina is one of the world's biggest producers and exporters of beef, wool, wine and wheat.

MANUFACTURING AND SERVICE INDUSTRIES

The manufacturing sector has grown in recent years and accounts for about 36% of Argentina's GNP. Close to one-fifth of the workers are employed in this sector of the economy. Argentina's industrial base is quite diverse. Thanks to the bounty of the pampas, the chief industry remains the processing of meat and other food products. Other industries include textiles, leather goods, chemicals, metals, printing, lumber, fishing, automobiles and railroad cars, and consumer goods. The country's factories are highly concentrated in and around Buenos Aires.

The service industries produce 55% of Argentina's GNP and employ about 57% of the work force. Workers in the service sector include those with jobs in the local, state and federal governments, the military, schools, hospitals, stores, restaurants and banks. Also of particular importance are workers in the fields of transportation and communications as their contributions help to build the infrastructure of the economy.

NATURAL RESOURCES

In addition to the rich, fertile soil of the pampas, the country has abundant natural resources. It has enough natural gas reserves to last at least another 60 years. An extensive pipeline system links the natural gas fields with important industrial centers.

Oil and hydroelectric energy sources are being developed. Petroleum supplies about 70% of the energy used in Argentina. The most important oil fields are located in Patagonia and the Piedmont. Argentina is one of the chief oil-producing countries in Latin America. Hydroelectric plants supply about two-fifths of the country's electricity.

Much of Argentina's mineral reserves still remain to be explored. Among the minerals found are beryllium, coal, copper, iron, lead, manganese, tin, tungsten and zinc.

Although there are large forest reserves, especially in the northeast and the south, the timber industry is still fairly small.

Investment in the development of the nation's resources has led to the recent digging of new quarries, mines, and oil wells. The building of additional roads, dams and factories has also fostered economic growth, new job opportunities, and the development of the rural areas of the country.

Oil towers are a common sight in Argentina. The country is self-sufficient in crude petroleum and petroleum products.

Below: **The hide of the cow provides leather from which shoes and jackets are made.**

IMPORTS AND EXPORTS

The export of agricultural products provides an excellent balance of trade. Argentina exports about two-thirds more than it imports. Its chief exports are grain, meat, wool, hides, vegetable oils, fruits, vegetables, nuts and manufactured goods. The countries that receive these goods include the United States, the Soviet Union, Italy, Brazil, Japan, and the Netherlands.

Argentina's chief imports are industrial chemicals, non-electrical machinery, transportation equipment, iron, steel and coffee. It imports chiefly from the United States, Brazil, Germany, Bolivia, Japan, Italy, and the Netherlands.

To further improve the balance of trade, Argentina strives to increase the production of export goods and to manufacture products locally rather than import them. It produces nearly all the consumer goods—such as cars, refrigerators, and television sets—that it once imported. One potential drawback of this policy is that it misses some opportunities to buy goods that are made more cheaply abroad, where labor costs may be even lower than in Argentina.

INFLATION AND FOREIGN DEBT

The people of Argentina have one of the highest standards of living in South America. Yet other figures tell a story of economic decline. In the 1920s, Argentina had the eighth-largest economy in the world. By 1987, its economy ranked 58th worldwide.

During the Perón era, the government gave the people extensive social welfare services. The social security system provides pensions upon retirement for all workers. It also provides health and maternity benefits, compensation for workers injured on the job, unemployment payments, and financial aid to the poor and the aged.

While these programs seem to help Argentineans live better, many economists blame runaway government spending for the spiraling inflation rate. At times, the government printed extra money to cover its expenses, thereby increasing inflation.

Through the years of political instability since Perón, the goals of economic productivity and efficiency have been all but ignored. Now state-run industries lose billions of dollars each year.

In 1989, the railroad system lost $2 million a day. The private business sector also depends on subsidies from the government and suffers from "feather-bedding," a term meaning jobs are provided for unproductive workers.

Inflation results in rising costs and a fall in the value of money. This resulted in many people becoming poorer as their salary and savings dropped in value.

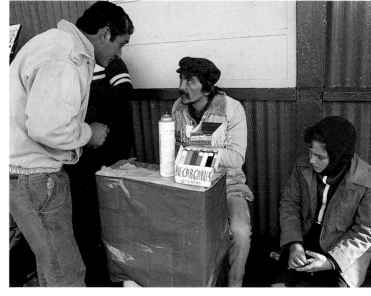

ARGENTINA IN THE 1990S

Yet Argentineans have grown comfortable with a system in which the government provides jobs for huge numbers of workers and subsidizes many businesses. It would mean a wrenching change for people to give up their guaranteed jobs and cradle-to-grave benefits in order to stabilize the economy.

Argentina faces continuing economic problems. The average annual income is $2,140. This low figure is the result, in part, of unemployment and wage controls meant to limit inflation. Inflation soared to a record high of 647% in 1984.

Each year, Argentineans could buy fewer real goods with their income than the year before. With mounting frustration, many Argentineans have watched their wealth decline in recent years. They are living poorly in a country with rich natural resources. Many workers worry about day-to-day economic survival. Some are holding down two or even three jobs to make ends meet. The very wealthy, who make up less than 1% of the population, have different concerns—primarily, fear of losing a lifestyle

The bus is slowly replacing the railroad which, in the early part of the 20th century, was used to transport people as well as livestock and agricultural produce to the ports.

of luxury based on the government's protection of their special interests. During the years of galloping inflation, it is estimated that wealthy Argentineans sent $30 billion to private overseas bank accounts.

As the 1990s began, Argentineans faced an uncertain economic future. President Menem's government pledged to undertake tough policies geared toward greater economic efficiency. It planned to sell off state enterprises, reduce the number of public jobs, withhold aid from failing private companies, raise prices for basic services, and balance the budget.

The government made plans to sell its national telecommunications company and a large part of the national airline to foreign buyers. These sales would wipe out more than $7 billion of the $62 billion foreign debt.

The transfer of state-owned companies to private owners is a dramatic change in policy from the Peronist party tradition of nationalizing the economy. The Buenos Aires electricity company, the oil industry, and some companies owned by the armed forces are also due to be sold to private owners in the near future.

The stock exchange in Buenos Aires. Slowly but surely, Argentina, one of the most resource-rich countries of South America, is on the road to recovery.

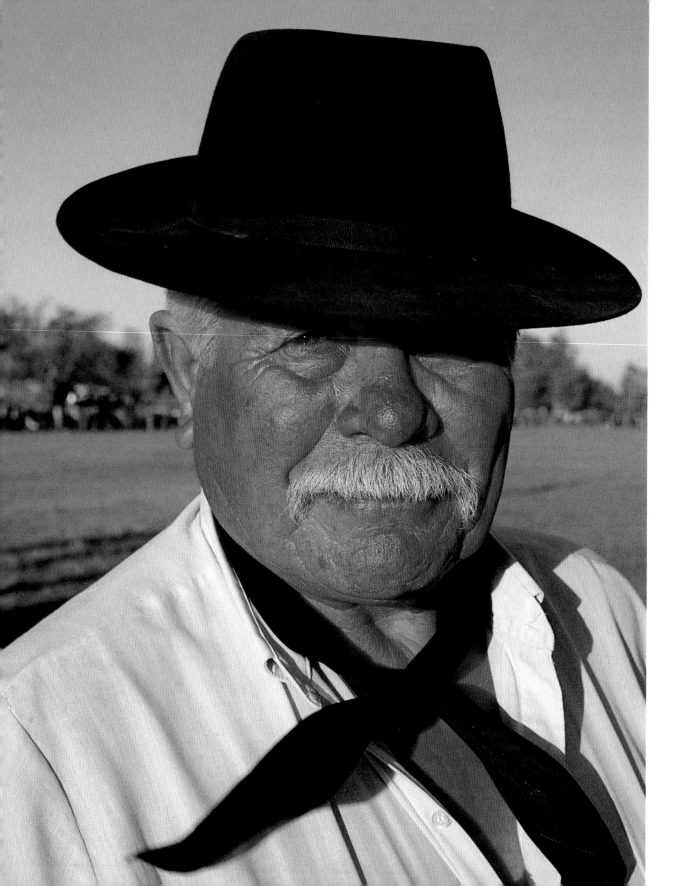

ARGENTINEANS

THE HEART OF ARGENTINA is its people, all 32 million of them.

One of the great surprises for visitors to Argentina is that the people don't look especially "South American." The high cheekbones, darker skin tones, and coal black hair of the native Indian population and the *mestizos* and mulattos, or mixed races, are not characteristic of crowds on the street. Instead, these people look European.

Many other countries on the continent have large populations of native American Indians, blacks of African descent, and mixed races. About 85% of Argentineans, in contrast, are whites of European descent. The remaining 15% are *mestizo*, Indian, and other non-white groups.

As people migrated from different parts of Europe, they tended to settle near others from their home country. Buenos Aires and other large cities and towns still have ethnic neighborhoods where the customs and special foods of European countries are preserved. Some of these groups publish newspapers in their own languages. They also run schools, hospitals, and clubs for their countryfolk.

Another surprise to visitors is that the largest group comes not from Spain but from Italy. About 4 out of 10 people in Argentina are from Italian families, while only about 3 out of 10 trace their families back to Spain. Most of the Italian immigrants settled in and around Buenos Aires.

Opposite: **Gauchos were once despised as being hard-drinking and rowdy. Today, they represent the desired qualities of an Argentinean: nobility, courage and great independence.**

Below: **Unlike children from other South American countries, these toddlers have very European features.**

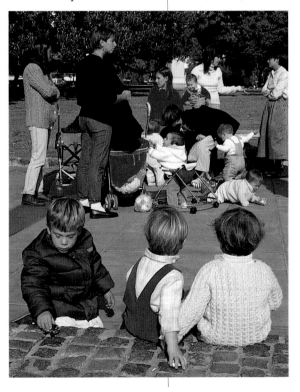

OTHER ETHNIC ROOTS

Argentina once had the largest community of British people anywhere in the world outside Britain. They were influential in developing the country's railway, telephone, electricity, gas, and steamship services. They brought sports such as rugby, cricket, polo and tennis, and imported cattle from England. Today their descendants are called Anglo-Argentines. The Falklands War between Great Britain and Argentina presented them with a potential conflict of loyalties, but most sided with Argentina.

The people came mostly from Italy, Spain, France, Russia, Germany, Britain, Poland and Wales.

The lure of new land has not dimmed. More than one million Europeans came following the Second World War. Europe's loss was Argentina's gain. Along with its Italian, Spanish, British and Welsh immigrants, Argentina is also enriched by people of Austrian, Dutch, French, German, Irish, Jewish, Polish, Portuguese, Russian, Swiss, Chinese, Japanese and Syrian descent. Immigrants have also come from neighboring South American countries, largely for political and economic reasons. Most recently, newcomers have arrived from Southeast Asia.

SOCIAL CLASSES

When the major waves of European immigrants arrived in Argentina, they found that the rural areas were controlled by large landowners. The newcomers could not easily own land or houses in the countryside, so they went instead to the major cities, especially Buenos Aires.

The cities enabled immigrants to find jobs, gain education, and become part of Argentina's middle class. For this reason, Argentina has a larger middle class than most other Latin American countries. The urban middle class includes workers in small businesses, as well as some government officials and professionals.

From the mid-1800s to the mid-1900s, political and social life in Argentina were shaped by the "landed aristocracy." These were the large rural landowners. Many had close ties to British people and their culture. Wealthy members of the upper class considered themselves among the world's most sophisticated, well-traveled and well-educated people.

The landed aristocracy used to have more power in the past. Now urban leaders of industry, commerce, and the professions, and military officers exercise considerable power in determining how the country is run. Social divisions are based on education, money and family background, and a certain amount of snobbery exists.

Among the wealthy today are ranchers, or *estancieros,* who own large tracts of land and herds of cattle but live in the cities. They often own other businesses in the towns while the farms and ranches are worked by hired hands.

Since the 1930s, large numbers of people have left the countryside to seek work in Argentina's larger cities. Many found only part-time work and have become part of a poor lower class that live in slum conditions.

THE PROUD GAUCHOS

The gauchos are a special group of men in Argentina who used to roam the pampas on horseback. Most were *mestizos*. A much smaller number still work as ranch hands on cattle ranches today. The gauchos of the past have become folk heroes and continue to inspire the culture of the country as a symbol of strength and individualism.

Like cowboys of the North American Wild West, the gauchos were excellent horsemen. They tamed wild horses, herded cattle and were skilled and courageous. They could find their way on the plains under any circumstances. By chewing grass, they could tell whether there was water near by and whether it was salt water or fresh. They could tell directions from the lie of the grass, or count the number of riders by their sound alone.

Gauchos often led rugged lives with few comforts. They lived in huts with mud walls and floor, a straw roof, no windows, and, frequently, an animal hide for the door. They were proud, self-reliant and tough. They fought for survival against the forces of nature and the native Indians. During colonial times, they opposed the authority of Spain. Later, they lived in opposition to the new settlers who fenced in their open range.

During the 19th century, their main job was to take cattle to the markets in Buenos Aires. The building of roads and railroads and the fencing-in of the *estancias* changed all that. Today, the gauchos still work in the open range driving tractors, repairing engines and vaccinating cattle against disease.

One costume that the world associates with Argentina is the dress of the gauchos. They are known for their thick leather belts, decorated with silver and sometimes with old coins.

Gauchos adopted the use of *bolas* from the Indians. A *bola* is a long rope ending in two or three pieces tied to hard balls covered with leather. Gauchos used it for hunting, especially the ostrich-like rhea. When thrown, it wraps around the legs of a running animal and ties it up. Several times in a year, during a rodeo festival, one could catch a gaucho exhibiting his legendary horsemanship skills.

The gauchos survived on a diet of meat and *yerba maté*, a holly tea. A typical picture of a gaucho shows him on horseback or at rest, singing and accompanying himself with a guitar, or sipping *yerba maté* through a metal straw from a hollowed-out gourd.

THE CRIOLLOS

In colonial days, the word *criollos* meant people born in Argentina of Spanish parents. Later, it came to mean descendants of early Spanish settlers, not families of 19th century European immigrants. Today, it can also mean a person who lives in the country or in a small town. The *criollos* who worked the land have provided much wealth for the country. *Criollos* are not racially mixed or foreign-born immigrants.

ANCIENT INDIAN TRADITIONS

The roughly 50,000 pure-blooded Argentinean Indians in the country tend to live in the isolated areas of the Andes, the Gran Chaco, Patagonia, and Tierra del Fuego. The Diaguita Indians, for example, live west of Salta at 9,800 feet. This area was part of the Inca Empire before the Spaniards arrived in the 16th century.

Although the soil is poor, the Indians farm the mountain-side, growing beans, corn and potatoes. They use irrigation channels built centuries ago by their ancestors to help in their farming.

Because the air is too thin at this altitude for cattle and

sheep to live, these Indians use llamas for meat, wool, and transportation. From the llama wool, the women weave clothing for their families, and socks, sweaters, scarves and blankets to sell to tourists.

Each Indian community has its own style of dress. The women's hairstyles also differ from one area to the next. The Diaguita people observe a mixture of Argentinean and traditional tribal customs.

Christianity merges here with ancestral beliefs. These Indians pray to gods of the sun, the moon, the earth, and also to the gods of thunder, rain and lightning.

Opposite above: **The Indians in Argentina remain economically limited as the lands within the Indian reservations are mostly barren.**

Opposite below: **An Indian girl. The Indians have the distinctively Asian features of their predecessors who crossed the Bering Strait to Alaska long ago.**

DISAPPEARANCE OF BLACKS

Argentina had a significant black population in its early years. These were the descendants of slaves imported from Africa by the Spanish in the 16th century. Argentineans of African descent constituted about 30% of Buenos Aires' population from 1778.

These people were slaves until the slave trade was outlawed in 1813. Most slaves were freed by 1827, but some didn't attain freedom until 1861. After the emancipation, most blacks continued to suffer from low status in Argentinean society.

Between 1836 and 1887, the percentage of blacks in Buenos Aires dropped from 26% to 1.8%. Historical paintings, prints, and photographs and the epic poem *Martín Fierro* revealed the presence of these Afro-Argentines, who are rarely seen today. Their disappearance from the country's society remains something of a mystery.

Some scholars believe that the majority of blacks died during the yellow fever epidemic of 1871, or in warfare, or disappeared through interbreeding with whites.

LIFESTYLE

THE ARGENTINEAN PEOPLE are still in the process of evolving a more unified culture. Their relatively short history of immigration resulted in many Argentineans keeping to the customs of their families brought from their country of origin. Also, the great variations in geography called for various ways of coping with life. The Welsh sheep-ranchers of Patagonia, the Indian farmers of the Andes, and the city sophisticates of Buenos Aires could not be more different from each other. For these reasons, there are many different lifestyles in Argentina.

Yet certain customs and traits are shared by most Argentineans. They are strongly nationalistic; they are pretty relaxed about punctuality. And they love to talk sports—especially soccer—and politics.

"The Argentines are still trying to figure out if they're European or Latin American, and they are famous throughout Latin America for not having made up their minds yet."
    —*Deirdre Ball*

FROM BIRTH TO DEATH

The traditions and customs of any society are usually influenced by their religion. The majority of Argentinean Catholics follow the practices of the church in observing important events in their lives.

Babies are usually baptized, and First Communion is celebrated around the ages of seven or eight. Girls have their first dancing party with boys when they are 15. This is society's recognition that they are now old enough to date boys.

When a couple becomes engaged to be married, they exchange rings. The woman wears her ring on the fourth finger of the right hand until the wedding, when she shifts it to her left hand. In the wedding ceremony, the groom walks in with his mother and the bride with her father. This custom symbolizes that both are leaving their families and joining as man and wife at the altar.

At the final event of the life cycle, death, a body may be either buried or cremated. It is quite unusual for the body of a dead person to be embalmed and viewed in an open coffin, as was done for Evita Perón.

FAMILY LIFE

Family life is very important to Argentineans. Families tend to be nurturing and supportive and they love to hear compliments about their home and children. This close bond among family members makes them fiercely loyal to one another.

Children are rarely sent away to boarding school; they are quite likely to live at home until marriage and then settle near their parents. University students generally attend classes in their hometown and continue to live with their parents. Workers often come home for lunch.

People care for their elderly parents and frequently invite a widowed parent to live with them. It is not common for the elderly to live in nursing homes.

The extended family of aunts, uncles and cousins has frequent reunions. This network of connections is often used to get into a better school or to gain a better job.

The father is often a strong authoritarian figure in the family. He also bears the chief responsibility for earning money to support the family, although many women also work and contribute to the family's income.

Young people live under the rules of their families and may feel controlled by them through their teen years and often until marriage or even longer.

The most outstanding traits of an Argentinean include a close bond with family and place of birth, a strong sense of patriotism and profound respect for tradition and culture.

CITY LIFESTYLE

The history of Argentina is marked by the contrast and sometimes the conflict between the city people and the rural people. In many ways, they have opposing views of life.

City life in Argentina reflects the European roots of an immigrant nation. The architecture and city plan—the layout of streets, parks and squares—have a European look. As in Spanish cities, the cathedrals and chief government buildings face the plaza, or main square. Argentina's artistic culture, organization of schools, fashion, business customs, and forms of polite behavior are very European oriented.

The Buenos Aires *porteños* are the leading city dwellers in Argentina. They dominate its government and cultural life. *Porteños* view themselves as sophisticated and up-to-date, and frequently set trends in behavior and fashion that later spread to the provinces.

Many *porteños* have little interest in visiting other parts of Argentina. They sometimes feel superior to people from the countryside and are accused of viewing anyone who doesn't live in Buenos Aires as one of the *campesinos* or country folk, even if that person happens to live in another big city.

Above and below: **The fashion-conscious look to Europe and to a lesser extent the United States for the latest trends in clothing and makeup.**

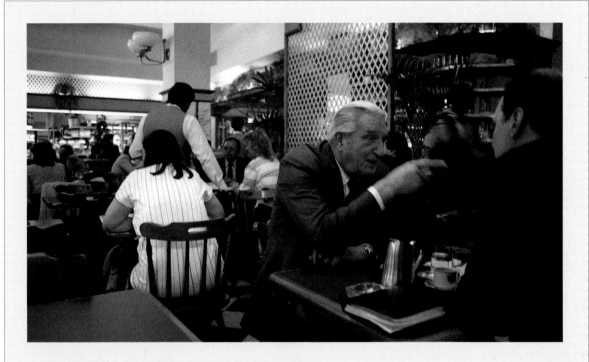

FRIENDSHIP THRIVES IN THE CAFE

Argentineans love to discuss sports, politics, philosophy and the arts. In Buenos Aires, especially, this means lingering in a café talking with friends. There are hundreds of old cafés that spill onto the busy streets. What one orders is less important than the relaxed atmosphere. The waiters never rush the customers. The English custom of tea-time and snacks in the afternoon continues in Argentina.

The Tortoni is the oldest traditional café in Buenos Aires, founded in 1858. It has a charming old billiard room, and the walls are decorated with presents from painters and writers who have gathered there over many decades. Conspirators and army chiefs have also come to sip coffee or play a game of chess. Jazz shows add to the attractions on weekends.

Cafés, restaurants, and clubs stay open very late. The typical work day runs from 9 a.m. to 7 p.m., or even as late as 10 p.m. Dinner may be scheduled for 10 p.m. or eaten as late as midnight. Some streets of Buenos Aires are bustling with people long after the clock strikes 12.

Because Argentineans are often creatures of habit, many prefer to meet over and over again at the same familiar café.

Bookstores offer a popular alternative meeting place for intellectuals. The favorite discussion, always, is what it means to be Argentinean.

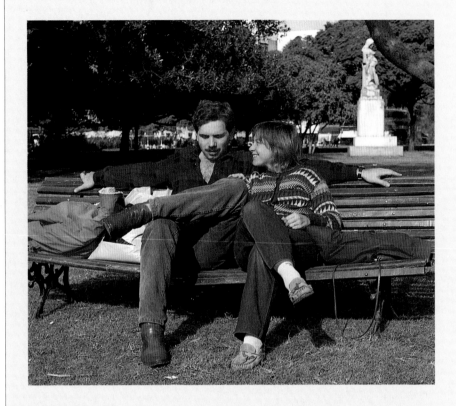

Opposite above: **Country house by the sea.**

Opposite below: **In the hilly and mountainous regions, the horse is still a common means of transport.**

THE SUGAR, SALT AND SPICE OF RELATIONSHIPS

The warmth of family ties is extended to friends. People tend to touch each other often while visiting together. They hug and kiss on meeting and leaving one another. When introduced, men shake hands, but close male friends may hug one another in greeting. Women who are friends shake hands with both hands and kiss one another on both cheeks.

Argentine flirting has a certain style. A man may pass a woman on the street and compliment her on her beauty without expecting her to stop or reply. His compliment, called a *piropo*, may be indirect: "It must be lonely in heaven since one of the more beautiful angels has descended to earth!" Less poetically, when passing a mature woman, the man might say: "Old but still good."

Women also flirt with witty remarks, even put-downs, to men that are meant to be heard and enjoyed by other friends.

COUNTRY LIFESTYLE

In the interior, European influences on lifestyle are less noticeable. Many living styles exist. Some people live and work on huge ranches, often built as luxurious country estates in the Spanish style of architecture. Others live on small farms. The poorest live in mud-and-straw homes with dirt floors.

Country people tend to see themselves as humbler, having more common sense, and being in better touch with the land than the people of the cities. They sometimes resent what appears to them as the self-centered arrogance of the *porteños*.

The great rivalry between the people of the interior and the people of Buenos Aires, once so heated, no longer erupts into violence. The two different ways of life are today increasingly seen as complementary to one another.

Above and below: **The rich live in luxurious houses, the poor in overcrowded, shanty towns known as *villas miserias*.**

RICH AND POOR

Another major contrast is between the lifestyles of the wealthy in Buenos Aires' northern suburbs and the poor who live in slums a mere bus ride away. Church and volunteer women's organizations have got together to raise money to build adequate housing for the shanty town residents of Tigre, a fading resort northwest of the city.

Charitable giving runs counter to the Argentinean tradition of avoiding taxes and other obligations to society. In the past, people had seen too much of their funds disappear into bribes, payments to unnecessary "middle men," and theft. The women volunteers need to assure wealthy donors that the money they give will truly reach the people it was intended to help.

POLITICAL TALK

Under the recent democratic governments, the Argentinean people have resumed their enthusiastic public displays of their political views.

In 1945, thousands of workers answered Evita Perón's call to protest her husband's detention by marching in the Plaza de Mayo. Historians mark that event as the day the working class gained real political power.

Street rallies, marches and people carrying placards are part of the traditional expression of political ideas in Argentina. Traffic halts for union demonstrators and students playing protest songs. Political graffiti can be found on many buildings and walls.

During elections, Argentineans will turn out in large numbers to vote at the polls. Most speak freely about which political party they support, and who they voted for in the last elections.

A street rally in Buenos Aires.

WOMEN

The women of Argentina are very deceptive. As nice housewives, they pretend they are soft, but they really rule the roost. They smile a lot, but they do what they want.

Traditionally, women in Argentina do not play a large role in public life. Evita Perón is especially admired by many feminists for her active role in promoting the rights of women. She worked to gain women's right to vote, and she advocated many rights for women workers.

Through her efforts, divorce was made legal, but this right was withdrawn shortly after her husband's fall in 1955. Not until 1987 was divorce legalized again.

Women have equal rights under the constitution. Since the 1940s, they

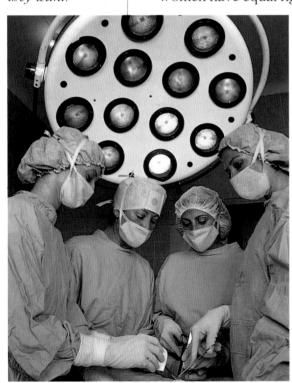

have become more active working outside the home. Women work as doctors, lawyers, architects, and in other professions. President Juan Perón's third wife, Isabel, became president of the country. Still, women are a long way from enjoying an equal role with men in business and government.

Women became forceful in public life during the "dirty war," when the courageous "Mothers of the Plaza de Mayo" marched each Thursday past the Casa Rosada carrying placards with the names of their missing loved ones. At great personal risk, they demonstrated to end human rights abuses and hold the government accountable for the "disappeared."

When a woman marries, she keeps her maiden name. If María García marries Juan Adler, she becomes María García de Adler or Senora García de Adler.

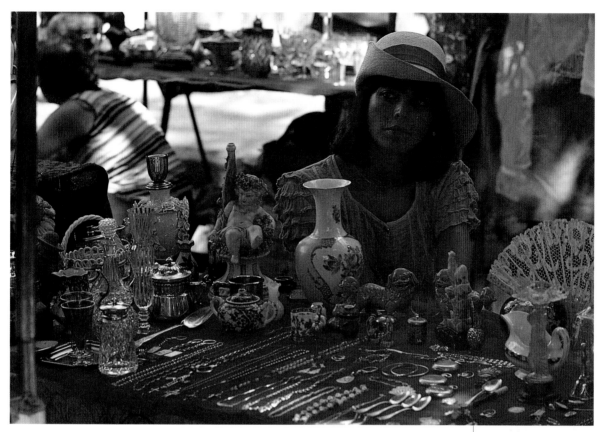

Letters are addressed not to "Mr. and Mrs. Juan Adler" but to "Mr. Juan Adler and Mrs.," which reads in Spanish *"Senor Juan Adler y Senora."* Children take the father's last name.

Although it is acceptable for women to go to restaurants and theaters alone, without a chaperone, women more commonly go out in groups. The physical abuse of women is not culturally accepted. Crimes of rape and incest are considered rare and are not frequently reported to doctors or police.

Teenage pregnancies and illegitimate children are also uncommon. Although it is a Catholic country, the knowledge and practice of contraception and abortion are common in Argentina.

ARGENTINEAN ATTITUDES

While some Argentineans go in for dramatic gestures, the general tendency is to avoid loud and unusual behavior in public. They don't like to call too much attention to themselves. Still, they may show their emotions, both happiness and sadness, with a Latin American openness of expression.

A relaxed time frame governs the leisure gatherings of friends. Dinner guests arrive 30 to 60 minutes after the specified time. When invited to a birthday party, guests bring gifts, which are usually opened in their presence.

Many Argentineans go to psychiatrists or psychoanalysts, and many of the analysts in Spain come from Argentina.

Argentinean Attitudes

Some think psychiatry is popular because people see themselves more as individuals than as part of a group. They tend to be quite concerned with their personal thoughts and feelings.

When you ask for directions on the street, an Argentinean may give a detailed answer rather than admit that he or she doesn't know. It's a point of pride for some to appear to know the right answer.

Some add drama to life or cover up their poverty with a bit of exaggeration. A woman may tell her friends that her car and driver brought her to the restaurant where they are meeting for lunch when, in truth, she came on the bus. A man may tell a new acquaintance that he lives in a building known for its expensive apartments when he actually lives in a more modest home.

As in other countries, Argentineans have ways of attracting good luck. One tango interpreter, for example, crosses herself and prays that each performance will be successful. Some performers wear lucky amulets or put on the same tie when they go on stage.

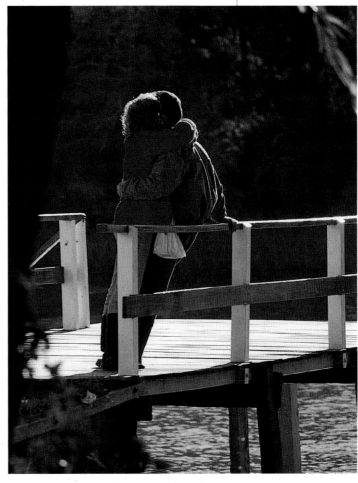

The people of Argentina are very open about their feelings and emotions, though they are more conservative than other South American cultures.

Right: **Telephone wires are not hidden underground but are exposed overhead. In the financial district of Buenos Aires, so many telephone lines are strung together they resemble a giant cobweb spreading above the city streets.**

Below: **Nightlife in Buenos Aires. Many restaurants in the cities are open till the early hours of the morning.**

SOCIAL AND BUSINESS CUSTOMS

Argentineans prefer to do business in person rather than over the phone. Appointments for business meetings are preferred to unexpected visits to an office.

It is polite to make small talk at the end of a business meeting, not to leave abruptly when the business is settled. Most Argentineans prefer not to discuss business during meals. The pace of negotiations is much slower than in the United States, for example, and is based more on personal contact.

Many people drop in on friends from around 4 to 6 p.m. without calling

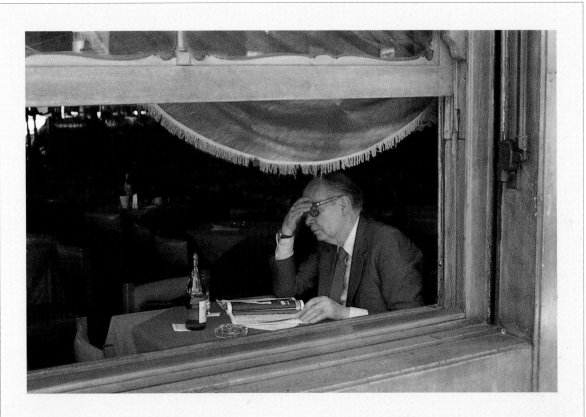

NOSTALGIA FOR THE PAST

Argentineans are said to have a sentimental streak. They remember the past in songs and stories, and in the glorification of the gaucho as folk hero. The architecture of the cities is full of reminders of the past—old fountains, wrought-iron gates, and countless other details. Families remember their immigrant past through collections of treasured photographs. Tango music expresses this nostalgia with lyrics that speak of lost loves and unfulfilled dreams.

ahead. Social plans are likely to be spontaneous, not scheduled weeks in advance.

Especially in Buenos Aires, people stay out late many nights of the week and seem to survive on little sleep. Shops are closed on Saturday afternoon, so that people may nap to rest up for Saturday night activities. Shops are also closed on Sunday, and families commonly gather for large noon meals.

RELIGION

ROMAN CATHOLICISM is the official religion of Argentina. The vast majority of the people, more than 90%, call themselves Catholic. In fact, less than 20% attend church regularly. In general, the people take a relaxed view toward religion. Still, when the Pope visited in 1982 and again in 1987, millions flocked to see their spiritual leader.

According to the constitution of 1853, the president and vice president must be Roman Catholics. The government also provides some financial support for the Church. The constitution guarantees freedom of religion for all people, and requires that strong relations exist between the Church and the state, but in an environment of religious pluralism and freedom.

Each religious group can maintain its own churches, hospitals, social centers and cemeteries. Religious schools are allowed, but religion may not be taught in the public schools. Religious faiths or sects can be banned if they appear to threaten public order and morality.

By law, all children must be registered at birth with names, usually biblical, that are in a registry of acceptable first names. These are often but not always names of Catholic saints in the Spanish language.

Within the Catholic Church are different groups, or orders, that do different kinds of work. Some run hospitals, some guide education, some try to convert non-Catholics, and some work with prisoners. In religious matters, monks and priests follow the directions of local bishops, who are guided by the Vatican.

Opposite: **There are many church buildings, grand and simple, in Argentina. Small town churches around the country are modeled after Spanish chapels.**

Below: **The grand and opulent architecture of the colonial churches bears testimony to the past wealth and power of the Church.**

OTHER RELIGIOUS GROUPS

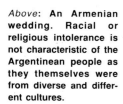

About 2% of the population today are Protestants. Besides Roman Catholics and Protestants, there are Christians belonging to the Armenian, Orthodox, and Ukrainian Catholic churches. Many Jews came from Europe in the late 19th and early 20th centuries. They number less than 2% of the population and live mostly in Buenos Aires. Moslems, spiritualists, sect members and atheists make up about 1.3% of the population.

Writers have called the reverence paid to Evita Perón a kind of religious fervor. After her death, her husband tried unsuccessfully to have the Catholic Church name her a saint. Her followers still place fresh flowers at her tomb every day. Believers ask her to grant their wishes and protect them from harm.

Religion is especially strong in the rural areas. The *mestizo* descendants of immigrants maintain elements of their Indian religions mixed with Roman Catholic beliefs and practices. They pray to nature spirits as well as to the Christian God. They have festivals throughout the year dedicated to the Indian gods; parties are filled with singing, dancing and feasting. Folk religion, blended at times with superstition, thrives away from Buenos Aires. Local shrines to unofficial saints are popular sites for pilgrimages.

About six weeks before Easter, at the beginning of the period called Lent, the yearly celebration of Carnival begins. In parts of Argentina, the decorations for Carnival are inspired as much by folk religion as by Christianity. Superstition blends with Christianity, for example, when a person makes the sign of the cross to ward off the "evil eye." Magical, occult and "new age" spiritualism find expression in Argentina, too.

YAMANA BELIEFS

The Yamana Indians, now extinct, were an ancient aboriginal people who lived at the southern tip of Argentina. Their stories were told but were never written down until a priest, Father Martin Gusinde, collected their legends in the 1920s from the last survivors. Myths about their people include a story of a great flood.

Lexuwakipa, a spirit-woman in the form of an ibis (a species of bird), felt offended by the people. In revenge, she let it snow so much that a huge mass of ice covered the earth. When it started to melt, it flooded the earth. The glaciation occurred at the time when men battled women, and succeeded in seizing their secret meeting place, which was the source of the women's power.

The water rose steadily and rapidly, and the people tried to save themselves. Finally, only five mountain peaks remained above water. After the water had remained level for two full days, it subsided. Practically all the Yamana had drowned. Only a few families had managed to save themselves. Once the great flood had subsided, those few survivors began to rebuild their homes. But ever since that time, the men have ruled the women.

Christ of the Andes. Situated on the Argentina-Chile border, the statue was erected to symbolize the lasting peace between the two countries.

MIRACULOUS STATUES

Incredible tales about miraculous statues often revolve around Argentina's churches. Here are but two of the more famous examples.

THE VIRGIN OF LUJAN In 1630, before the town of Luján existed, a man tried to drive an ox cart carrying a statue of the Virgin Mary over the place where the church now stands. But the cart just could not be moved. No matter how many oxen were hitched to the cart, the statue still remained at the same spot. The people decided that the Virgin Mary did not want her statue to leave that spot.

They unloaded it and built a small chapel for it. A large, richly decorated church was later built for the thousands of pilgrims who come to Luján each year to pray to the Virgin. Luján is about 44 miles west of Buenos Aires.

THE CRUCIFIX OF SALTA In the 17th century, a statue of Christ on the cross was being shipped to Salta Cathedral from Spain when the ship carrying it sank in a storm at sea. Miraculously, the statue floated to the coast of Peru. It was then carried by a horse across the Andes to Salta, a distance of 1,600 miles.

There were great celebrations when the statue arrived safely. After the festivities it was packed and stored away in the cathedral cellar.

One hundred years later, a major earthquake shook Salta. The people went to the cathedral to pray. They heard a voice saying that the earthquake would not stop until the statue was put in its proper place in the cathedral. The statue was brought out and paraded around the city before being returned to the cathedral. The earthquake stopped. Since then, the statue has been paraded around the city each year to celebrate the event.

LANGUAGE

JUST ABOUT EVERYBODY in Argentina speaks Spanish, the official language of the country. Spanish is taught in virtually all the schools and is the only language used by the government.

The Spanish used throughout Argentina is full of local variations. Some dialects are so different from the Spanish of Spain that speakers from both places might have trouble understanding one another.

The many people who came from Italy have changed the language greatly, giving an Italian sound to the pronunciation of some words and adding other words from the Italian language.

The Italian influence is most noticeable around Buenos Aires and in the pampas, where many Italians settled. The Italian greeting *buongiorno* often replaces *buenos días,* the Spanish "hello". "Goodbye" becomes *chau,* a variation of the Italian *ciao* (pronounced "chow").

In Argentina, the sound of "ll" in words like *cordillera,* meaning "mountain range," is pronounced "sh." In other parts of South America, "ll" sounds like "y."

The *mestizos* in the north use dialects influenced by Indian languages. Immigrants from Mexico, Bolivia, Chile and Paraguay, and their descendants, speak in distinctive dialects of Spanish.

Opposite: **Reading is a favorite pastime, and books and magazines can be easily purchased everywhere.**

The many immigrants and Indian tribes have lent great variety to the local dialects used in Argentina.

OTHER VOICES

English is spoken throughout Argentina as a second language. Other languages, such as German, are still spoken by immigrants in the larger towns and cities. Welsh is spoken by descendants of the Welsh immigrants in Patagonia.

Only a small number of the remaining Indians in Argentina still speak Guaraní, Quechua, or other Indian languages. The names of these disappearing languages are quite musical: Aymará, Chiriguano, Chorotí, Mataco, Mocoví, Toba, Lule, Ranquel, Moleche, Tehuelche, Ona … Scholars are beginning to preserve the legends and traditions that will disappear when the people who speak these languages die out.

OF GANGSTERS AND TANGO SINGERS

A special language related to tango music, popular songs and the theater is called *lunfardo*. This dialect has influenced the Spanish spoken in Buenos Aires since around 1900. *Lunfardo* uses words borrowed from Italian, Portuguese and many other languages.

Lunfardo began as a slang of criminals. Words were borrowed, invented and used in a way that could only be understood by themselves. *Lunfardo* playfully changes the names of things. For instance, to speak of a person's head, the *lunfardo* speaker might choose words that mean "a bed of fleas," "thinker," "ball," or "the top of a building."

Soon poets and journalists discovered the colorful expressions of *lunfardo* and began to use them in their writing. Tango singers also began to use them in their songs. From 1916 on, poets wrote works in *lunfardo* with such titles as *Versos rantifusos* (Street Verses) or *La crencha engrasada* (Slicked-Down Hair). The first tango to be sung had *lunfardo* lyrics and was called *Mi Noche Triste* (My Night of Grief). It was sung in 1917 by Carlos Gardel, the most famous of all tango singers.

For a period of time beginning in the 1940s, the use of *lunfardo* was banned. Nevertheless, it continued to enrich the spoken and written language of Buenos Aires. As with all slang, new words are added and old ones dropped over the years. In 1962, a group of scholars, artists, and radio people founded the Lunfardo Academy of Buenos Aires to preserve and polish this distinctive language.

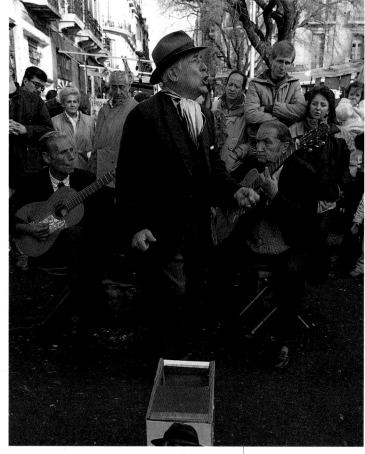

The tango singer expresses himself in the language of *lunfardo*.

DID YOU KNOW…?

The Argentinean people tend to speak fast and pronounce some consonants differently from the Spaniards in Europe. Some "s" sounds in Argentina are pronounced "th" in Spain. The Castilian Spanish of Spain sounds almost as if the speaker is lisping to a person used to the sound of the English language. In Argentina, the "ll" sound is like a soft "j" or "sh." In other Spanish-speaking South American countries such as Chile, "ll" sounds like a "y."

When Spanish is written, question marks (?) and exclamation marks (!) appear not only at the end of a sentence, but also before the first word, upside down.

In Spanish, the meaning of a word can change depending on which syllable is stressed. *Papa*, with the stress on the last syllable, means "father." *Papa* with no stress on the final syllable means "potato."

There is no "a.m." or "p.m." in the Spanish language. To say 8 a.m., a speaker must use words that translate to "eight in the morning." Airports, and train and bus stations usually use a 24-hour clock. When it is 3 p.m., these clocks read "15:00."

ARGENTINEANS LOVE TO READ

With their country's high literacy rate, Argentineans read many newspapers in Spanish and foreign languages. At least 230 newspapers are published, about 70 in Buenos Aires alone. *La Prensa,* known for its excellent coverage of international news, and

The Spanish speaking tourist may find difficulty understanding the local Spanish spoken on the streets.

La Nación are two important dailies, both over 120 years old. The *Buenos Aires Herald,* founded in 1876, is the most important English-language newspaper in South America. Newspapers published in Buenos Aires are sold in most of the country. Major provincial cities also have their own newspapers. The oldest in print is probably *La Capital,* founded in Rosario in 1867.

The degree of freedom enjoyed by the press has varied under different political regimes. *La Prensa* was seized by Juan Perón's officials in 1949, and was not returned to its owners until 1955. Publications have been banned because they were considered immoral or pro-communist by the government. In 1976, a period of book censorship began, and scholars were persecuted for their ideas. The present government allows the press and writers freer expression of ideas and criticism.

Colorful streetside stalls selling magazines and newspapers are a common sight in the cities.

More than 4,000 books and periodicals are published each year. The first magazine in Argentina, *La Ilustracíon Argentina,* was printed in 1853. Picture magazines such as *Gente* and *Siete Días* are very popular. Among the best-known literary ones are *Ficción, Sur,* and *Nosotros.* Readers browse through the country's 8,000 bookstores, many of which are open for 24 hours a day.

RADIO AND TELEVISION

Argentina has more than 100 radio stations and numerous television stations. Buenos Aires alone has one private and three state-owned stations. It is estimated that there is one radio in use for every 1.5 persons and one television set for every 5.2 persons. In comparison, the averages for the United States are two radios per person and one television per 1.7 persons. Many television programs are imported from the United States and dubbed in Spanish.

EDUCATION AND LITERACY

Almost everyone in Argentina can read and write as schooling has been made compulsory for all children.

Argentina has an astonishing 94% literacy rate. Education is free from kindergarten to university. Children attend seven grades of elementary education. This requirement is generally obeyed, even where rural schools are hard to reach.

The school year runs from March to December in most parts of the country. Teaching is in Spanish, but English, French and Italian are taught beginning in elementary school. Elementary students may wear white coats over their own clothes. In many junior high schools, the students wear uniforms.

Although high school education is not compulsory, there are free government and fee-charging private schools in most cities. They offer five years of classes. Only a small percentage of students finish secondary school.

There are more than 50 public and private universities. The University of Buenos Aires is the largest, with more than 100,000 students. The University of Córdoba is Argentina's oldest, founded in 1613. Because many students work full-time, night courses are quite popular. The three most popular careers are architect, political scientist and doctor.

Public schools owe their success largely to President Domingo Faustino Sarmiento (1868–74). He enlisted the advice of a famous United States educator, Horace Mann. Still, Argentina's public school system was modeled most closely after the French system. These schools later helped to "Argentinize" the children of immigrants.

PROVERBS WITH A SPANISH TWIST

Some proverbs take on a different flavor in a different language. Here are some English proverbs and the English translation of the Spanish version:
- English : Too many cooks spoil the broth.
  Spanish : A ship directed by many pilots soon sinks.
- English : Don't count your chickens before they're hatched.
  Spanish : Don't eat the sausages before you kill the pig.
- English : A bird in the hand is worth two in the bush.
  Spanish : A bird in the hand is worth a hundred flying.
- English : You cannot make a silk purse out of a sow's ear.
  Spanish : You can't find pears on an elm tree.
- English : Much ado about nothing.
  Spanish : Much noise (of cracking), few nuts.

(SOURCE: *Native Tongues* by Charles Berlitz)

GUARDIA VIEJA
TANGO
ISRAEL HOFFMANN
1896 – 1971

THE ARTS

IF THE HEART OF ARGENTINA is its people, the soul of the country is its artistic culture. Outstanding artists have created works of international interest in dance, music, drama, literature, painting, sculpture and architecture. Argentina's creative center is greater Buenos Aires. *Porteños* support fine museums, theaters, art galleries, and opera, symphony and dance companies. The larger cities around the country also have thriving libraries, museums, theaters and concert halls.

Argentinean art quite often reflects international styles and ideas. Churches, homes and civic buildings recall their counterparts in Spain, Italy and France. Much popular music pays homage to jazz, disco and rock music from the United States.

The outside world has long since recognized the power and originality of Argentinean artists. They have persisted through periods of political repression; some were forced into exile while others courageously continued to work in their homeland. The return of democracy to the country in the 1980s sparked a cultural revival in all the arts.

Partly because there are few Indians to influence the culture of Argentina, folk arts and crafts are not as prominent as in other South American countries. A blend of Indian and Spanish traditions shapes the woodcarvings, bolos, ponchos, *maté* (tea) sets, handwoven fabrics, hammocks, costume jewelry and other handicrafts produced today.

Opposite: **Everybody knows Argentina to be the Land of the Tango.**

Below: **Paintings for sale in a market. Most artists are strongly influenced by European art.**

ART THROUGH ARGENTINEAN EYES

The earliest artistic expressions on view in Argentina are cave paintings and engravings, some small stone heads, and a carving of a human foot with six toes.

The archeological remains and pre-Columbian menhirs—tall stone columns—in Tafí del Valle in Tucumán province are particularly striking. Early natives created circles of incised stones, and dozens remain in this valley that was sacred to the Diaguita tribes. Tall standing stones from this region, some 10 feet high, have been collected in Menhir Park. Scholars cannot agree on their age or the meaning of their mysterious inscriptions.

Prehistoric ceramics of the Condorhuasi culture are of strange figures with animal and human characteristics.

After the arrival of the Spanish and through colonial times, religious themes dominated artistic expression. Manuel Belgrano founded the School of Geometry, Perspective and Drawing in Buenos Aires during the colonial period.

Two early Argentinean painters in the 1830s were Carlos Morel and Fernando García Molina. Prilidiano Pueyrredón and Cándido López dominated painting of the 19th century. Benito Quinquela Martín and Uruguayan-born Pedro Figari depicted the life of Buenos Aires in more recent times.

Art movements orginating in Europe, such as impressionism, appealed to many Argentinean painters. Much current work expresses art for its own sake rather than as social commentary. As in other countries, some artists have blurred the distinction between photography, painting and sculpture. The visual and dramatic arts are sometimes combined in performance pieces.

Among the noteworthy artists who have worked in clay, stone or ceramics are Lucio Fontana and Fernando Arranz. The sculptures of Julio le Parc and Alicia Peñalba are widely known outside Argentina. A teaching photographer, Pedro Luis Raota, has won awards in at least 22 countries.

Argentina's artists show their work in more than 100 art galleries in Buenos Aires and additional galleries and museums in the smaller cities.

Opposite above: **Indian handicrafts. Although Argentina's Indian civilization did not reach the artistic heights of the Incas in neighboring Peru, it still produced beautiful and highly artistic crafts.**

Opposite below: **A sculpture in the park. In the bigger cities, sculptures and murals are located in public for everyone to see and appreciate.**

Below: **Mural on the wall of a building.**

GAUCHO ART

The uniquely Argentinean theme of gaucho life has inspired literature, painting and music.

Gaucho handicrafts. These handicrafts, the spurs, the knife and the *bolas,* tell us of the type of life the gaucho leads.

Domingo Sarmiento, the country's president from 1868 to 1874, attacked the legend of the proud, rebellious gaucho in *Civilization and Barbarism: Life of Juan Facundo Quiroga* (1845). He felt that education, not rebellion, was the key to the country's future. *El Gaucho Martín Fierro* (1872), a famous epic poem by José Hernández, described in vivid detail the difficult life of a gaucho. This masterpiece, called the "national poem," is still read in school. Hernández's portrait was sympathetic to the plight of the gauchos. He portrayed the people they encountered and often fought with—Indians, blacks, the military and the police—and the forces threatening their way of life.

Novelists influenced by Hernández included Benito Lynch and Ricardo Güiraldes. Güiraldes' *Don Segundo Sombra* (1926) imaginatively portrayed the decline of the gaucho. A group of young writers in the 1920s, known as the *Martinfierristas*, published a literary review called *Martín Fierro.* Jorge Luis Borges, a member of this group, emerged as a nominee for the greatest prize in literature—the Nobel Prize.

The "father of Argentinean national music," Alberto Williams, composed a piece called *Aires de la Pampa* in 1893. One of the best known 20th century composers, Alberto Ginastera, used gaucho dances and songs in many of his compositions.

THE WRITTEN WORD

Many Argentinean writers came to the attention of the outside world when Victoria Ocampo spent a personal fortune to publish their works in the literary magazine *Sur,* which she founded in 1931. She also published short stories and poems of outstanding foreign writers, and her magazine enjoyed an international circulation.

Noted 20th century Argentinean writers include Leopoldo Lugones, Manuel Ugarte, Alfredo Palacios, Ernesto Sábato, Julio Cortázar, Manuel Puig, and Adolfo Bioy-Casares.

Italian-born Alfonsina Storni became a leading Argentinean poet. Bioy-Casares collaborated with Jorge Luis Borges and also wrote books on his own, including a chronicle of *porteño* life called *Asleep in the Sun.* Cortázar is known for short stories and novels, such as *Rayuela,* that have been translated into many languages.

Celeste Goes Dancing is an engaging sample in English of stories written in the 1980s by 14 representative Argentinean writers.

Jacobo Timmerman, a newspaper editor, gained international attention with his book *Prisoner Without a Name, Cell Without a Number* (1981). After he had been treated brutally by the military authorities, Timmerman accused them of attacking him not only because he expressed dissent against the government but also because he is a Jew.

A secondhand bookshop. Here one can exchange books or buy old books at a fraction of their real price.

JORGE LUIS BORGES (1899–1986)

Probably the most famous Argentinean writer, Borges' essays, poetry and short stories inspired an entire generation of writers. He was admired especially for his brilliant use of language and his original thoughts about the meaning of life. Borges' stories convey a sense of mystery, puzzles and the fantastic. Critics have compared them to the stories of Edgar Allan Poe.

Borges' international outlook may have sprung from his family roots. His father was of Italian, Jewish and English backgrounds, while his mother was Argentinean and Uruguayan. He studied

in Switzerland and published his first poem in Spain. He disapproved of Perón but took no active part in politics. In 1927, Borges began to lose his vision, and by age 56, was completely blind. Through the help of assistants, books and writing remained the central passion of his life. At 68, he wed for the first time, but the marriage was unhappy and did not last. Shortly before his death, he married his 41-year-old secretary and traveling companion.

Among his best-known books available in English are *Ficciónes* (Fictions) and *El Aleph* (the aleph is the first letter of the Hebrew alphabet). Borges won many literary honors, including Spain's most important literary award in 1980. He was nominated several times for the Nobel Prize in literature but never won it.

Opposite above: **The most famous tango singer was Carlos Gardel. From 1917, when he invented the tango song, to his death in the 1930s in an airplane crash, Gardel grew into a national hero. His music is as popular today as it was during his lifetime.**

Opposite below: **The tango in motion.**

MUSIC AND DANCE

Composers in Argentina have been influenced by both European models and songs of the gauchos. Jesuit missionaries taught music to the native Indians in the 17th century. Amancio Alcorta (1805–62) is considered to be the first native-born Argentinean composer. Through the years, many composers, singers, instrumentalists, conductors, dancers and choreographers from Argentina have achieved international standing.

Opera, so beloved by Italians, is second only to the tango in popularity. Among the best-known works is Alberto Ginastera's opera *Bomarzo,* remembered for its violence and dramatic impact on audiences. More than 70 Argentinean operas have been produced at home and abroad.

Folk dancing thrives in provinces such as Salta. Many of the best folk dancers are still in their teens. Dance styles echo Inca, Spanish, gaucho and other Latin American forms of music and dancing

ARGENTINA'S TANGO The music everyone identifies with Argentina is the tango. As a dance, the tango is characterized by a male and female dancer holding each other and gliding together in long steps, in between pauses in dramatic poses. The accompanying lyrics are often melancholy musings on lost love.

The tango appeared near the end of the last century and gained worldwide popularity early in the 20th century. Some scholars trace its roots to gypsy music in Spain, while others say it developed from the *milonga*, an earlier dance popular in Argentina, and from other dances such as the polka. Tango music is generally played by guitar, violin, flute, piano, or especially the *bandoneon,* a relative of the accordion. People who dance it are called tango interpreters.

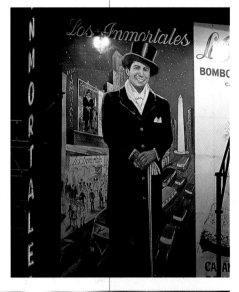

Beginning as a means of expression for the lower classes, the tango was at first considered vulgar by the upper classes. In the 1920s, the Pope declared that there was nothing sinful in dancing the tango. Its popularity spread to the upper classes in Buenos Aires and then to other countries around the world. Tango is now performed mostly for tourists.

MUSEUMS AND SCIENTISTS

The National Museum of Fine Arts opened in Buenos Aires in 1896, and soon became a showcase for the works of local artists. Today it houses works of modern Argentinean and foreign artists, as well as 400-year-old paintings illustrating Argentinean history.

Other museums in Buenos Aires include the Museum of Spanish-American Art, with its valuable collection of colonial artifacts and silver, and the Pharmacy Museum, where antiques from apothecaries are on display. The José Hernández Museum specializes in the culture of the gauchos. The city of Rosario has an excellent Museum of Modern Art. In La Plata, the Natural Science Museum, founded in 1877, has a world-famous fossil collection. Many fossils housed there came from the pampas and Patagonia, discovered by Florentino Ameghino (1854-1911), one of the world's first paleontologists.

FILM

The movie industry in Argentina developed after the First World War. Buenos Aires and Mexico City became the chief producers of films in the Spanish language.

Argentinean movies have won awards in film festivals in many countries. In the United States, *The Official Story* won an Oscar for Best Foreign Film (1985). Actress Norma Aleandro was nominated for Best Actress in that film. She portrayed a woman who discovers that her adopted daughter is the child of one of the "disappeared." A film based on Argentinean Manuel Puig's novel, *Kiss of the Spider Woman,* won the Academy Award for Best Motion Picture in 1986. This film again reported on the official persecution of private citizens. In spite of a thriving local film-making industry, movies imported from the United States and Europe are still the most popular in Argentina.

When they are not outdoors playing games, Argentineans love to read, dance and go to the movies.

Right: **The Córdoba University is a beautiful example of colonial architecture. Built in 1613, it was the first university in Argentina.**

Below: **The Teatro Colón is one of the world's largest and most elegant opera houses. Built from 1887 to 1908, it is considered the finest concert hall in Latin America.**

ARCHITECTURE

Colonial architectural styles are especially well preserved in northern Argentina. A handsome example is Córdoba's cathedral, completed in 1784. Like the cities in Spain, most towns in Argentina are built around a main square. The cathedral and chief government buildings face this plaza. In the countryside, many lavish estates were also built in the Spanish style.

Buenos Aires shows the influence of Spanish and Italian architecture, but many visitors feel it resembles Paris most of all. Wide boulevards, apartment buildings with balconies, and large government buildings dating from the 19th century remind visitors of the French capital. Numerous gardens, many containing marble statues, add to the beauty of the city.

BENITO QUINQUELA MARTIN AND LA BOCA

If one artist could change the look of a city, painter Benito Quinquela Martín is just the sort of person. He built a primary school for the children of La Boca, formerly a slum area of Buenos Aires. When he gave the school to the city, it was on condition that it also house a museum of waterfront paintings. As a result, La Boca became an art colony, with Quinquela Martín as one of its most talented painters.

He also persuaded a number of restaurant owners in La Boca to paint their buildings in bright colors. Owners of run-down homes in the neighborhood followed suit, painting them in vivid red, yellow and blue. He also established an open-air market to promote local artists.

This river-front section in the city remains a favorite gathering spot for painters, sculptors and poets. Tourists enjoy the colorful buildings and restaurants. Spirited music in the clubs reminds them that the tango first appeared in the dance halls of La Boca.

LEISURE

ARGENTINEANS ENJOY a climate that favors outdoor activities throughout the year. The name Buenos Aires comes from the early Spaniards' gratitude to the Virgin of the Good Winds for their safe arrival in this delightful land. Today, Argentineans are still grateful for good winds and fresh air near their beautiful lakes and rivers, the Atlantic Ocean, and the majestic Andes mountains. They camp, hunt, fish, hike, climb rock faces and mountains, ski, sail, windsurf, cycle, and play tennis, squash and golf. They take seaside vacations on the Atlantic coast and inland vacations in resort areas such as Bariloche.

Besides these individual and family pursuits, Argentineans love team sports. They play them and watch them, cheering for their favorite teams and players. You'll find them watching everything from basketball and cricket to rugby and soccer, all games with international appeal. They also enjoy rugged contests on horseback, some unique to Argentina. Unlike many other Latin American countries, however, Argentina does not support the dangerous sport of bullfighting.

Opposite: **Clowns in the park. Argentina is blessed with a cool and refreshing climate that favors outdoor activities.**

Below: **The rock pools at Iguazú Falls are good bathing and wading areas.**

A PASSION FOR SOCCER

Probably the most popular sport in Argentina is soccer, known as *fútbol*. The English brought this game to Argentina in the last century.

Children grow up playing soccer at school, in the street, or in any open space. Competition to make a boys' team is fierce, and those boys

The dream of every Argentinean child is to be rich and famous by becoming a football superstar.

who grow up to become professional soccer players earn top salaries. They often become national heroes.

In Buenos Aires, a traditional rivalry pits the Boca Juniors, from the Italian neighborhood of La Boca, against the River Plate team. Three-quarters of the nation's fans support one of those two teams.

Among national teams, a passionate rivalry exists between Argentina and Brazil. More than 100,000 fans will turn out to watch a game between the two countries.

Some of the country's best soccer players leave to play for the wealthier club teams of other countries, especially in England, Spain and Italy. Brazil and Mexico also hire Argentinean players. Still, these soccer stars often return home to compete for Argentina in the World Cup championship games.

Argentina's soccer honors include the Junior World Championship in 1979 and the World Cup in 1978 and 1986, when they defeated Holland in their first triumph and West Germany in their second. In the 1990 tournament, after defeating archrivals Brazil, and a favored Italy, they lost to West Germany in the Finals. Sergio Goycoechea, the substitute goalkeeper who stepped in as replacement in the final matches, became a national hero with his superb and inspirational play.

SMALL BUT MIGHTY

Argentina's Diego Maradona is today considered the best soccer player in the world. His fiery personality, tremendous athletic skill and performances have made him the subject of many stories. The 5-foot-5-inch star from the Villa Fiorito slum in Buenos Aires has been called everything from Argentina's "Golden Boy" and "king of soccer" to "explosive," "vulgar," "spoiled," and "Mr. Disagreeable." He wears No. 10 on his jersey, traditionally given to a team's best scorer; it is also the number of soccer's greatest star, Pele. And like Pele, his life is a rags to riches story.

Maradona currently plays as an attacking midfielder for Napoli in Italy. He has a $23 million contract, and is said to earn another $8 million a year in endorsements and business income, making him one of the world's highest-paid soccer players. He makes headlines frequently about his weight, missed training sessions, and threats of leaving Napoli. His most notorious exploit, though, occurred during the 1986 World Cup, when he scored in a 2-1 win over England by knocking the ball into the goal with his fist, later attributing it to "the hand of God."

In polo, players on ponies try to hit a wooden ball with their sticks into goals at either end of a 295-yard-long playing field. Four players are on a team, and the game has five or six periods, called *chukkers*.

BRITISH HORSEBACK

The gaucho tradition of great horsemanship still influences Argentinean sports. The game of polo, played on specially-bred ponies, was brought by the British and flourished in Argentina.

In Buenos Aires alone, crowds of 20,000 routinely turn out to cheer for their favorite players, such as Gonzalo Pieres, a national hero and ranked as one of the world's best.

Players begin their training as children, swinging little mallets from bicycles. Then they play in leagues like those for soccer. The best polo players own farms where they can practice all year round. Family teams of fathers and sons, uncles and cousins are common.

Prized for their speed and ability to work with their riders, Argentinean polo ponies may cost up to $5,000 apiece.

Show-jumping is another sport in which local riders and horses have won international attention. Both the National Polo Fields and the famous Argentine Horsetrack are in Palermo, a northern suburb of Buenos Aires. Argentineans love to go to horse races. To cater to this interest, a newer turf race track has been built in the Buenos Aires suburb of San Isidro.

GAUCHO HORSEBACK

A game on horseback called *pato* originated with the gauchos. *Pato* was originally played using a live duck (*pato* in Spanish). The duck was placed in a sack with its head sticking out. Two teams raced over a three-mile-long field fighting over the sack. The frequently bloody fights that ensued led to the banning of the game in 1822. But it came back under President Juan Manuel de Rosas. Today, a six-handled, inflated leather bag replaces the duck.

To score points, players must land the bag in a netted iron hoop three feet in diameter at the opponent's end of the playing field. *Pato* has mostly been a working-class game, but its popularity is spreading among other social groups. As in the more upper-class game of polo, horses are valued for their speed, strength, endurance and ability to work with their riders.

In the game of *sortija,* a horseman gallops at full speed and tries to place a short lance through a ring hanging from a bar. Much skill is needed as the ring may be the size of a wedding ring.

Rodeos are popular in many parts of Argentina, with roping and riding contests where descendants of the gauchos demonstrate their traditional skills. The most important rodeo is held each May at Ayacucho.

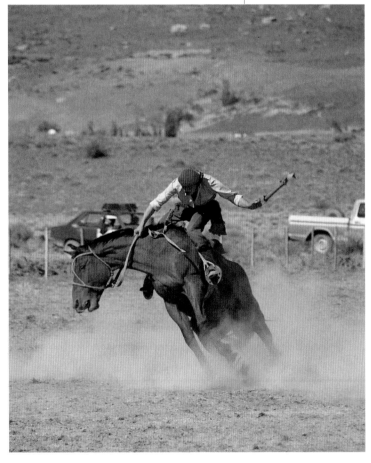

99

RACING LEGEND JUAN FANGIO

Like soccer star Diego Maradona, Juan Manuel Fangio was born under poor circumstances but acquired international fame and wealth through competitive sports.

In the 1950s, when Fangio won the Grand Prix championship five times, the lives of racing drivers were both glamorous and risky. Drivers wore neither hard helmets nor flame-proof clothing. Thirty drivers—all Fangio's friends—died in flaming wrecks during that decade. Because cars today have better brakes, wider tires and more safety features, there are far fewer fatal accidents.

In his autobiography, Fangio devotes an entire chapter to the topic of luck. He believes that "no one dies before the day that is marked." He has been accused of being cold-blooded, and, in fact, old newsreels show him driving skillfully past burning wrecks that roll into screaming spectators. "When someone was killed, I thought to myself, surely he committed an error," he has said. Fangio trusted his skills, his mechanics and his cars. He had two accidents in which his co-driver died. He blamed those crashes on his lack of sleep.

Fangio grew up poor and worked long hours from childhood in a garage. Perhaps it was there that he gained the mystical ability his competitors said allowed him to communicate with the steel, engines and tires of his cars. His first race was in a 1929 Ford taxi, but he later won driving Alfa Romeos, Mercedes, Ferraris and Maseratis. He retired while still on top and became president of Mercedes-Benz in South America. In 1990, at 79, he is still honorary company president for life, going to the office each day in spite of having undergone five heart surgeries. Fangio founded an auto museum in his hometown of Balcarce, where 500 of his trophies and 50 of his racing and classic cars are on display.

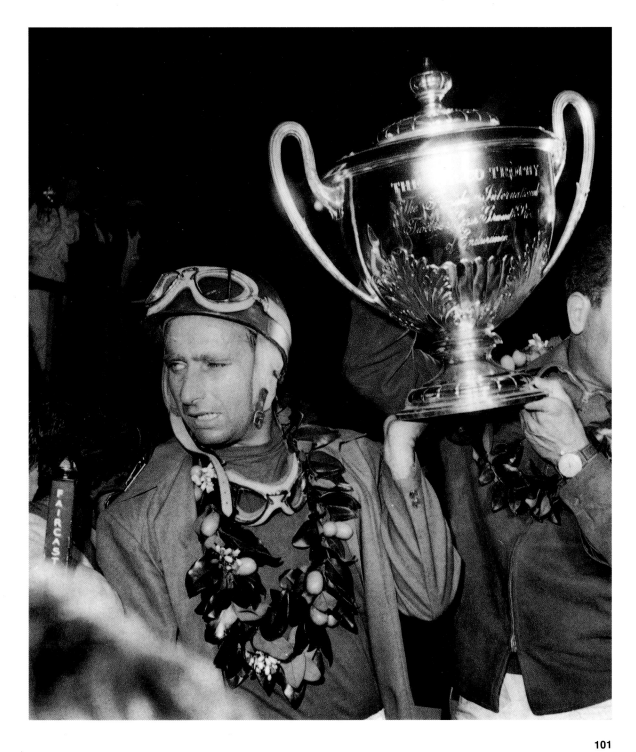

SCALING THE HEIGHTS

In early August, a snow carnival and the annual national ski champion-ships are held in Bari-loche.

Mountain climbers from many countries come to Argentina to attempt to scale the Andean peaks. Mendoza, about 800 miles west of Buenos Aires, is the chief province for mountain climbing.

Mt. Aconcagua, the highest peak in the Western Hemisphere, provides the ultimate challenge. It was first climbed by Matias Zurbriggen of Switzerland in 1897. There are 10 recognized routes up this mountain, but most climbers use the northern route. Teams from West Germany, Italy, Switzerland and the United States have climbed here. The mountain has claimed many lives; climbers who died on the mountain are buried in a small cemetery at its foot.

For people who prefer to go up and down with the help of wings, another adventurous sport, gliding, is rather popular. It is sponsored by the Air Force. International competitions are held in the hills near Córdoba, an area of challenging wind drafts.

COMPETITIVE SPORTS CREATE HEROES

As the passage on Juan Fangio reveals, professional auto racing is a much-loved sport in Argentina. While Fangio was a world champion driver five times, other Argentineans have taken over his mantle, like Carlos Alberto Reutemann, a famous Grand Prix driver, and Ricardo Zunino, who already has a top reputation in this field.

Of the well-known Argentinean boxers, the most famous is probably Luis Angel Firpo, who fought in the 1920s. He was called "The Wild Bull of the Pampas" and is honored with a statue in Buenos Aires. He once knocked world heavyweight champion Jack Dempsey out of the ring in 1923 but lost that match. Other Argentinean boxers have been world champions in various weight classes, including Carlos Monzón, who held the middleweight title from 1970 to 1977.

Among the many titles and trophies won by Argentinean athletes are the world championship ice hockey title in 1978, many swimming records, golf and marathon running awards. Argentina's international tennis stars include Guillermo Vilas, José Luis Clerc, Ivanna Madruga and Gabriela Sabatini. Rugby star Hugo Porta is viewed as one of the greatest players of all time.

Fishing becomes competitive when national and international championships are held in Bariloche each year. A record 36-pound trout was caught in that region. Competitions are also held each year in Pas de la Patria, a town on the Paraná River in the northeast. People try for the largest golden Dorado, a fighting fish that can weigh up to 60 pounds.

Argentina has produced several chess world champions. Youthful stars have included world juvenile champion Oscar Panno in 1952, Carlos Bielicki in 1957 and world cadet champion Marcelo Tempone in 1979.

FESTIVALS

ARGENTINA IS ALIVE with festivals, or *fiestas*. Their colorful processions brighten the landscape from one end of the country to the other. Many different groups of people express their artistic, musical, and culinary creativity through festival celebrations. Argentinean festivals reflect the spiritual traditions of both native Indian religions and Christianity.

Argentineans remember historical events in some festivals. For example, each provincial city celebrates the anniversary of its founding. In other festivals, the people celebrate legends and myths of the many cultures that have enriched Argentina.

Festivals and holidays may involve religious pilgrimages, feasts, parades, dancing and even gaucho competitions on horseback. Most of the competitors in gaucho events are descendants of gauchos. They use traditional old costumes and saddles for the contest. A noted example, the Gaucho Festival of San Antonio de Areco, 80 miles north of Buenos Aires, takes place November 10 to 17.

Traditions of immigrant communities form the basis for some festivals. A noted one in October, the Welsh singing festival, takes place near Esquel, in the Patagonian mountain town of Trevelin. A gathering of Welsh poets and musicians also takes place each year at Gaiman in Patagonia.

Opposite: **Santa Claus in Buenos Aires. Christmas is widely and joyously celebrated in this Catholic land.**

Below: **No parade would be complete without the crisp display of marching soldiers.**

WINE, MATE, WHEAT AND PONCHOS

Some festivals celebrate the chief products of a region. In Mendoza, the wine-growing area along the Andes, the Vendimia Festival is celebrated to mark the grape harvest in March. It honors more than 1,500 wine producers from that part of Argentina. It is one of the most impressive festivals in Latin America. The vines are blessed, fountains of free red wine are available to the thirsty crowd, a festival queen reigns, and an impressive parade is held. The people of Mendoza also celebrate their history. Toward the end of February, before the wine festival, the whole region commemorates General San Martín's crossing the Andes.

In Posadas, the capital of the province of Misiones, there is an annual festival to celebrate the harvest of the *maté* crop. *Maté*, pronounced "mah'tay," is a kind of holly brewed to make a tea that is so popular it's considered the national drink. Ornately decorated coaches carrying the prettiest girls from each district of the province parade through the streets. One of the girls is chosen to serve as the year's *maté* queen.

The most important wheat festival in Argentina takes place in Leones, in the province of Córdoba. A wheat queen reigns over the commercial and industrial fair with its related folk events. People in the central farming provinces celebrate many harvest festivals.

The Fiesta del Poncho in Catamarca features the local production of handwoven ponchos. The fleece for these objects comes from three animals that can live at high altitudes: the alpaca, the llama and the vicuña. The people who proudly display their ponchos are continuing an ancient tradition. The gauchos wore ponchos as an indispensable part of their clothing. Today, tourists prize them for their artistry as well as their usefulness.

May 25, Independence Day. People dress in costumes and masks of the early 19th century to re-enact the Declaration of Independence.

CARNIVAL

Carnival occurs at the same time as similar celebrations among Roman Catholics all over the world, including the Mardi Gras in the United States. The celebration of Carnival in Argentina is especially vigorous in the northern part of the country. Business comes to a halt as costumed Argentineans dance in the streets.

Carnival festivities usually begin on the weekend before Ash Wednesday, which most often falls in February. The celebrations are mixed with Indian traditions in the northeast. In Tilcara, floral arrangements representing the Stations of the Cross are hung along the streets. Processions come down from the mountains on Ash Wednesday.

In many parts, Carnival is not celebrated with the same abandon as in Brazil. But visitors may find that the majority of people will party and that business and social life are far from normal during Carnival. Celebrants may be expected to finish a large cup of alcoholic drink in one gulp. They also may be doused by water balloons. They will encounter balls and parties in the hotels and clubs of major cities.

The yearly Carnival traditionally represents the people's last opportunity to make merry before earnest fasting and praying begins during the season of Lent.

The Tango Festival begins in the first half of January and kicks off a series of fiestas all across the country.

REGIONAL FESTIVALS

Every month of the calendar has its share of colorful regional festivals. In Puerto Madryn, an underwater fishing festival kicks off the New Year. In Rosario del Tala, a Tango Festival runs through the first half of January. The last half of January is devoted to a two-week National Folklore Festival in Cosquín in the province of Córdoba. An artisan fair held at the same time adds to the festivities.

On February 2, processions on horseback at Humahuaca near Jujuy bring pilgrims to the Candelaria Virgin. Fireworks, traditional foods and religious music add to the celebration. Northern Argentineans meet with southern Bolivians during the Easter week to trade handicrafts and other goods and again on the last two Sundays in October at the *Manca Fiesta* (Festival of the Pot), where merchandise is once more traded.

Salta Week, June 14–20, marks the anniversary of a local battle. While San Martín was fighting the Spanish, Salta's town hero, General Martín

Miguel de Güemes, led a band of gauchos against the Spanish in the Gaucho War. This festival includes fireworks displays, colorful floats, singing and dancing. Salta is also noted for its Christmas performances, tableaus and carol singing that go on for weeks.

Corrientes, which has a particularly lively Carnival celebration, marks its founding on May 3 with a religious and popular arts festival.

On June 24, St. John's Day is celebrated in several towns, most unusually in Formosa, where the faithful walk barefoot over a bed of hot coals. Processions in Salta, Jujuy and Mendoza honor St. James each year on July 25. St. Ann is honored a day later in Tilcara, near Jujuy.

Argentineans also enjoy gathering for the annual Livestock Exhibition in July at the Argentine Rural Society in Buenos Aires. Cattle, horses, sheep and pigs are judged for prizes and sold at auctions.

Historical events are celebrated throughout the country with much pomp and ceremony.

The small village of Villa General Belgrano hosts an Alpine Chocolate Festival each winter and an authentic Oktoberfest.

Several times during the year, thousands of Catholics make a pilgrimage to celebrate the Fiesta of our Lady of Luján, the patron saint of Argentina. Many walk from their homes all the way to Luján. Early in December, old coaches from a provincial colonial museum in Luján parade around the town, with the people dressed in colonial costume.

109

MUSICAL CELEBRATIONS

The northwest of Argentina is famed for its beautiful colonial architecture as it was one of the earliest Spanish settlements in Argentina. At the same time, it remains, till today, the heart of Indian culture. The region's history has contributed to the unique, present-day musical celebrations which fused both Indian and Spanish traditions.

The traditional customs of the Indians are still preserved in colorful celebrations like the *misachicos,* the carnival of Jujuy and some other religious festivals.

During these occasions, musicians will come down from the hills to crowd the narrow and steep streets of the white villages. They bring their *erkes* (a long trumpet with a distinctive sound which can easily be heard from places a long distance away), *charangos* (an instrument made from the carcass of a regional animal called the *mulita)* and typical bass drums.

Folk music is still alive in Argentina.

The music of the people who lived here long before the Spanish arrived survives in these celebrations with their merry songs and dances. *Carnavalitos, bagualas, zambas, cuecas and chacareras* are some local musical expressions, played with typical indigenous instruments like *erkes, charangos,* bass drums, *bombos, sikus* and *quenas,* mixed with some other European instruments such as guitars, violins and large accordions.

TWO INDEPENDENCE DAYS

The long-standing rivalry between the people of Buenos Aires and the people of the provinces has resulted in Argentineans celebrating two national Independence days.

May 25 marks the date when the people of Buenos Aires threw off the Spanish yoke. The people of the interior are honored by the holiday on July 9, when deputies of the interior Congress of Tucumán declared the United Provinces free. Now people in the capital and in the countryside celebrate both holidays.

During the May 25 celebrations a lavish and exciting parade would be held. The city plaza would be filled with army officers in riding boots, naval officers in 19th century frock coats and spats, and soldiers, massed in battle gear and black berets, in a re-enactment of the struggle toward nationhood. Regal gauchos ride on horseback, the proud symbol of Argentina, their red cloaks flowing in the wind.

PUBLIC HOLIDAYS

Official public holidays include both religious and historical commemorations.

Jan 1	New Year's Day.
Jan 6	Epiphany.
Apr	Good Friday, Easter Sunday and Maundy Thursday.
May 1	Labor Day.
May 25	Anniversary of the Revolution of 1810.
Jun 10	Malvinas Day—commemorating the Falklands War.
Jun 20	Flag Day.
Jul 9	Independence Day.
Aug 17	Anniversary of the death of General José de San Martín, the liberator of Argentina.
Oct 12	Columbus Day.
Dec 8	Catholic feast of the Immaculate Conception.
Dec 25	Christmas.

FOOD

IN ARGENTINA, THE SAYING GOES, everyone is an expert in barbecuing. And no wonder. Beef is by far the most popular food and some people eat it three times a day.

Traditionally, meat was spit-roasted in the courtyard of the home or in the fields. It was often impaled on a cross-shaped spit, one end of which was driven into the ground at an angle to keep the roast over the flames. At other times, it was cooked on a grill over hot cinders.

Today, the average Argentinean consumes 190 pounds of beef every year. Writers have attributed the overwhelming popularity of beef to a belief that eating it gives people the animal's vitality, and that people must eat plenty of it to be strong. Perhaps the real reason so much beef is eaten is that it is plentiful and cheap. Many people consider Argentinean beef the best in the world, tender enough to be cut with a fork.

The typical meal today is grilled beef, with french fries, salad and red wine. In restaurants, beef is served in hearty portions. Some restaurants place a small stove at each table and barbecue the meat in front of hungry customers. The meat is salted before it reaches the table.

It is not unusual for workers to choose one of their number to go to the butcher. He buys fresh meat which they roast or grill and share for lunch.

Slowly Argentineans are digesting news that eating less meat may lower cholesterol levels and improve health. But they enter the 1990s with the favorite diet still being beef and more beef.

Opposite: **An ice cream seller doing his acrobatic act for the camera.**

Below: **Beef is so popular in Argentina that they usually barbecue a whole cow over an open fire.**

Argentineans having a feast and a good time over the buffet plate.

ARGENTINEAN MEAL

Aside from the predictable main course, side dishes can have an Argentinean flair. *Matambre,* meaning "hunger killer," is an appetizer of marinated flank steak stuffed with spinach, hearts of palm, ham, or hard-boiled eggs and then baked. It is eaten hot or cold.

Lettuce and tomato salads are dressed with oil, often olive oil, and vinegar or lemon juice. The creamy and cheesy salad dressings of the United States are rarely used.

Desserts include fresh fruit and cheese and the much-loved *dulce de leche,* milk simmered with sugar until very thick. This sweet concoction serves as the base for other, more complicated desserts.

Alfajores con dulce de leche is a confection with two layers of dough surrounding a filling, with a coating over all. Each section of the country has its own style. Happily for "chocoholics," the chocolate versions are plentiful and delicious. *Dulce de leche* is also spread on breakfast toast, eaten by the spoonful, served along with ice cream, and used in cakes and meringues. Sometimes it goes with cheese to cut the sweetness. Sometimes it's spread on top of *flan,* a custard similar to the French *crème caramel,* making that dish even sweeter.

Rice pudding and *almendrado,* ice cream rolled in crushed almonds, also satisfy the Argentinean sweet tooth. Italian-style ice creams abound. *Dulce de membrillo* is a thick quince preserve sliced and served with cheese. *Dulce de batata* is a sweet potato preserve served thickly sliced.

Apples, pears, and grapes from Patagonia join citrus fruits from farther north on the dessert plates as well.

As in parts of Europe, coffee is often served espresso-style, brewed very strong and served in a small cup. In home entertaining, people may move from the dining room to the living room for coffee and an after-dinner brandy or other liquor.

A customer bargaining with the local fruit seller. Oranges are grown in the country.

Above: **A typical meal consists of grilled beef, salad, french fries and red wine.**

Opposite top: **A man cooking *empanadas*. Such snacks are handy for a quick bite between meals.**

Opposite bottom: **The Italian connection. Pizzas have been adopted as part of the local diet in the cities due to the large inflow of Italian immigrants.**

INTERNATIONAL INFLUENCE

The food of Argentina is really Italian, Jewish, Spanish, Polish, German and Chinese food. Only the Indian dishes can be considered truly native. The rest of "Argentinean cuisine" arrived with immigrants and reflects the many different ethnic groups in the country.

The gauchos contributed the *asado,* beef roasted over an open wood or coal fire. Argentinean variations on beef include: *bife a caballo* ("beef on horseback")—steak topped with fried eggs*; carbonada*—stew of beef, corn, squash, and peaches baked in a pumpkin shell; *churrasco*— grilled steak; *ossobuco*—beef stew; *chorizos*—spicy sausages; and *morcillas*—blood sausage from German and Polish cooking.

At the *parrillada,* a grill house that cooks meats over charcoal fires, one can order a *parrillada mixta,* or mixed grill. Some Argentineans enjoy heaping on the grill an assortment of sausages, short ribs, and organ meats such as kidneys, liver, and sweetbreads, and even the cow's intestines and udder.

From Europe comes *milanesa,* thinly-sliced beef covered with beaten egg and bread crumbs and then deep-fried. Besides beef, Argentineans eat roasted or grilled pork, goat and lamb. Spanish cooking inspired *puchero de gallina,* a chicken stew made with corn, sausages, potatoes, and squash. Children especially like *ñoquis,* which are potato dumplings served with meat and tomato sauce. Argentinean *empanadas* are derived from Britain's Cornish pasties. They are fried or baked pastries in a crescent shape, stuffed with chopped meats, cheese, creamed corn, other vegetables, fish or seafood. Chopped hardboiled egg, olives, raisins and onions sometimes flavor the filling

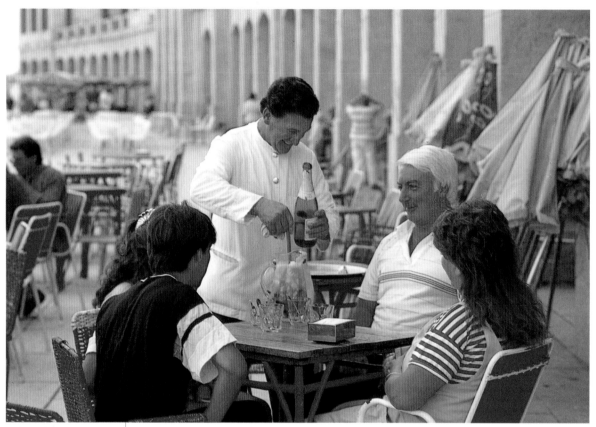

A family enjoying one of the fine outdoor cafés along the Mar del Plata.

With its thousands of restaurants, Buenos Aires offers a range of French, Chinese, German, Jewish, Iranian, Pakistani and many other ethnic foods. *Porteño* diners who venture beyond the grilled beef restaurants enjoy everything from Swedish smorgasbord and Swiss fondue to vegetarian meals.

Because of the Italian influence, both pizzas and pastas are numerous. Pizzas come with thin or thick crusts and a variety of toppings, including eggplant and artichoke. Other Italian cooking tends to reflect the regional styles of Naples and Sicily. Spanish paellas are also served at Argentinean tables.

Further south, Bariloche is known for its chocolates, fondues and strudels. The Welsh around Puerto Madryn in Patagonia operate many small tea houses that serve high tea with distinctive rich cakes, bread and jam.

NATIVE FOOD

One of the few truly native dishes to be found in Argentina is *locro,* a soup or thick corn stew. *Locro* contains beef, beans, potatoes, peppers, onions and lots of other ingredients.

The Indian influence on food is most noticeable in the north. In the northeast, near the famous Iguazú Falls, typical Guaraní dishes include *chipa,* a small, hard biscuit made of manioc (a starchy vegetable), eggs and cheese.

Sopa Paraguaya is a pie made of corn, cheese and eggs. *Reviro* is made of dried meat, onions and spices fried together.

In the northwest, too, certain dishes reflect the *mestizo* heritage. *Humita en chala* is a mildly spicy corn meal tamale cooked in corn husks. *Quesillo con miel de caña* is a soft cheese covered with sugarcane syrup.

Sweets and candies of all shapes and colors can be found along street-side stalls.

FINDING FOOD

Eating out is a favorite activity in Argentina. There are many types of restaurants and shops that cater to hungry diners. The great majority of restaurants feature beef. Some seat hundreds of people and are busy morning, noon and late into the night. People linger for hours over a three-course meal with orchestras entertaining them.

Outdoor cafés and restaurants are very popular in Argentina because of its pleasant climate

Sidewalk cafes line the wide boulevards of Buenos Aires. Argentineans take advantage of a moderate climate by lingering at outdoor tables as they take an English-style afternoon tea break.

The names of food shops sound like pure poetry … *pizzerías*, *cafeterías*, *heladerías* for ice cream, and *confiterías* for cakes, sandwiches, *empanadas*, and simple main dishes. *Confiterías* stay open from breakfast through to the midnight snack. Because most restaurants offer the same menu at both lunch and dinner, the *confitería* is the place to go for a light noonday meal.

Porteños tend to eat a light breakfast, a large lunch between noon and 3 p.m., late-afternoon tea and pastry, and a huge late dinner between 10 p.m. and midnight. Restaurants usually stay open until 2 a.m.

WINE AND OTHER SPIRITS

The wines of Argentina are considered some of the best in South America. Argentina produces its own beer, whiskey, rum, vodka, and other liquors, but it exports only its wines. The wines of Mendoza are well-loved throughout the country. Most Argentineans drink red wine with their meals. A highly-prized type is called Malbec. White wines are produced in the Salta region and are exported even to Germany.

Chilean wine is also served in many restaurants in Argentina. Wine and champagne coolers with fruit mixed in by the bartender are popular summer drinks. A slightly alcoholic cider, called *sidra,* is featured at the famous Café Tortoni. *Whiskerías* are numerous in Buenos Aires. These informal cocktail lounges also serve sandwiches. In general, the people of Argentina tend to chat over coffee or a soft drink rather than over cocktails. While they love to drink wine with meals, Argentineans also enjoy their food with carbonated mineral water.

Inside a rural *whiskería,* a bartender chats with his lone customer.

Maté cups and containers come in various shapes and sizes.

YERBA MATE

Maté (pronounced mah'-tay) is a type of tea made from the young leaves of an evergreen tree of the holly family known as Brazilian holly. The tea leaves come both from trees grown on plantations and from trees growing wild in the Misiones jungles. Also known as "Paraguayan tea," this drink is commonly called *yerba maté*.

To prepare it, the greenish herb is ground to the size of ordinary tea leaves. The leaves are steeped in very hot water in a gourd or bowl and then drunk from a small hole in the top through a metal straw called a *bombilla*. The straw has a filter to keep the leaves out of one's mouth. The bowl and the *bombilla* may be ornately decorated, often with silver. *Yerba maté* was developed by the native Indians, adopted by the gauchos, and finally taken over by the entire country.

In home parties, *maté* may be served plain or with sugar, anise seeds, orange peel or milk. The drink is sometimes shared socially, passing from person to person. Like regular tea, it contains some caffeine. The gauchos found it pepped them up and helped them to go for long stretches without food or sleep.

A *yerba maté* plantation.

A | B | C | D

Tropic of Capricorn

BOLIVIA

C H I L E

JUJUY

PARAGUAY

B R A Z I L

S A L T A

FORMOSA

CATAMAR

SANTIAGO
DEL
ESTERO

CHACO

Iguazú Falls

MISIONES

Río Paraná

CORRIENTES

Río Uruguay

LA RIOJA

SANTA
FÉ

SAN
JUAN

Córdoba
•

Salado

2

Aconcagua ▲

• Mendoza

CÓRDOBA

SAN
LUIS

ENTRE
RÍOS

URUGUAY

MENDOZA

**Buenos
Aires** •

Río de la Plata

LA PAMPA

BUENOS AIRES

3

P A C I F I C   O C E A N

NEUQUÉN

Río Colorado

Río Negro

RÍO NEGRO

Nahuel Huapi

Río Chubut

S O U T H   A T L A N T I C   O C E A N

4

CHUBUT

SANTA CRUZ

IS. MALVINAS

5

N
↑

TIERRA DEL FUEGO

• Ushuaia

ARGENTINA

Aconcagua B2

Bolivia B1
Brazil D1
Buenos Aires C2

Catamar B1
Chaco C1
Chile B1
Chubut B4
Córdoba B2
Corrientes C2

Entre Ríos C2

Formosa C1

Iguazú Falls D1
Is. Malvinas C5

Jujuy B1

La Pampa B3
La Rioja B2

Mendoza B2
Misiones D1

Nahuel Huapi B3
Neuquen B3

Pacific Ocean A3
Paraguay C1

Río Chubut B4
Río Colorado B3

Río de la Plata C2
Río Negro B3
Río Paraná C1
Río Uruguay D1

Salado C2
Salta B1
San Juan B2
San Luis B2

Santa Cruz B4
Santa Fé C2
Santiago del Estero C1
South Atlantic Ocean C4

Tierra del Fuego B5

Uruguay C2
Ushuaia B5

International Boundary
State Boundary
Tropic of Capricorn
▲ Mountain
● Capital
● City
River

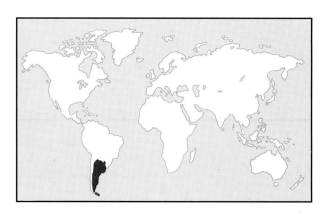

QUICK NOTES

LAND AREA
1,073,400 square miles
(400,000 square miles additional territory in dispute)

POPULATION
32 million

CAPITAL
Buenos Aires

PROVINCES
Buenos Aires, Catamarca, Chaco, Chubut, Córdoba, Corrientes, Distrito Federal, Entre Ríos, Formosa, Jujuy, La Pampa, La Rioja, Mendoza, Misiones, Neuquen, Río Negro, Salta, San Juan, San Luis, Santa Cruz, Santa Fé, Santiago del Estero, Tierra del Fuego and part of Antarctica and South Atlantic Islands (national territory), Tucumán.

HIGHEST POINT
Mt. Aconcagua (22,831 ft.)

LONGEST RIVER
Río de la Plata

NATIONAL ANTHEM
Himno Nacional Argentino ("Argentine National Anthem")

NATIONAL FLOWER
Flor de Ceibo (Flower of Ceibo Tree)

NATIONAL LANGUAGE
Spanish

MAJOR RELIGION
Roman Catholic

CURRENCY
Austral, divided into 100 centavos
Value against dollar changes periodically

MEASUREMENT
Metric system; temperatures in degrees Celsius

MAIN EXPORTS
Meat, wheat, corn, oilseed, hides, wool, fruits, nuts

IMPORTANT ANNIVERSARIES
Labor Day, Constitution of 1853 (May 1), National Day, Anniversary of the 1810 Revolution (May 25), Malvinas Day commemorating Falkland Islands War of 1982 (June 10), Flag Day (June 20), Independence from Spain in 1816 (July 9), Death of General José de San Martín (August 17), Columbus Day (October 12)

POLITICAL LEADERS
General José de San Martín—liberator
General Manuel Belgrano—served in revolutionary army; created the national flag
Bernardino Rivadavia—first President of Argentine Republic (1826–27)
Domingo Faustino Sarmiento—President (1868–74) and a noted writer; contributed greatly to public education
General Juan Perón—influential former President, (1946–55) and (1973–74)
Carlos Saúl Menem—President (1989–)

GLOSSARY

criollo	Person born in Argentina of European parents.
estancia	Large cattle ranch.
gaucho	Cowboy of the pampas, usually *mestizo*.
mestizo	Person of mixed European and Indian ancestry.
pampas	Flat grass plains of central Argentina.
pato	Sport played on horseback throwing a six-handled leather ball into a net.
porteños	People of the port city of Buenos Aires.
quebracho	Hardwood tree.
yerba maté	Holly tea sipped through a metal straw from a gourd.

BIBLIOGRAPHY

Hernández, José: *The Gaucho Martín Fierro*, Editorial Pampa, Buenos Aires, 1960. Adapted from the Spanish and rendered into English verse by Walter Owen with drawings by Alberto Guiraldes.

Huber, Alex: *We Live in Argentina*, The Bookwright Press, New York, 1984.

INDEX

Picture Credits: